ALPHABETS
AND
HIEROGLYPHIC CHARACTERS
EXPLAINED;

WITH AN
ACCOUNT OF THE EGYPTIAN PRIESTS,
THEIR CLASSES, INITIATION, AND
SACRIFICES,

IN THE ARABIC LANGUAGE
BY AHMAD BIN ABUBEKR BIN WAHSHIH;

AND IN ENGLISH
BY JOSEPH HAMMER,
SECRETARY TO THE IMPERIAL LEGATION
AT CONSTANTINOPLE.

ISBN: 978-1-63923-692-3

All Rights reserved. No part of this book maybe reproduced without written permission from the publishers, except by a reviewer who may quote brief passages in a review to be printed in a newspaper or magazine.

Printed: February 2023

Published and Distributed By:
Lushena Books
607 Country Club Drive, Unit E
Bensenville, IL 60106
www.lushenabks.com

ISBN: 978-1-63923-692-3

TRANSLATOR'S PREFACE.

The original of this translation was found at Cairo, where it had escaped the researches of the French *Savans,* who, though successful in collecting many valuable Oriental books and manuscripts, failed in their endeavours to procure a satisfactory explanation of the Hieroglyphics. Literary, as well as military, acquisitions excite great interest. After the harvest of the members of the French Institut, the less expectation there was of gleaning with success in the field of Egyptian literature, the greater satisfaction a discovery

TRANSLATOR'S PREFACE.

like this must give, and the more the acquisition of such a manuscript, equally new and interesting, deserves to be appreciated.

The account of its contents and author is as follows:—The author lived a thousand years ago, in the time of the calif *Abdul Malik Bin Marwán*. His surnames would be sufficient to prove that he was a *Caldean, Nabathean*, or perhaps a *Syrian* by birth, if he did not tell us himself that he translated a work treating on the hieroglyphics and secrets of Hermes, from his *mother-tongue*, the *Nabathean*, into Arabic.

Ali Abdur-rashíd Alba-koyi informs us in his Geography of Egypt (extracts of which are given by citizen Marul in the Egyptian decade) that in the year two hundred and five and twenty of the Hegira, a book was found in Egypt containing a notice of the construction of the pyramids and other Egyptian antiquities, written in unknown characters, and translated at last by a monk of the convent of *Calmoon*. This discovery proves to

TRANSLATOR'S PREFACE.

be coeval with the time our author wrote his book, which was finished in the year two hundred and forty one.

It is very likely that he had the means of perusing this translation of the Monk.

He deposited the original of the book before us (as we are acquainted by himself) in the library of the calif above-mentioned. This prince (one of the most enlightened of his dynasty) rivalled his great predecessors *Hárún Arrashíd* and *Mámún* in the encouragement given to the progress of the sciences, and to the translation of mathematical and philosophical works from the Greek and Syriac into Arabic.

Chalabizaade Hadshi Khalfa, the great Oriental encyclopædist and bibliographer, gives us in his Bibliographical Dictionary an account of the works of our author, and mentions him as one of the most celebrated translators that ever enlarged the empire of Arabic literature by precious translations from foreign languages.

Having thus made the reader acquainted with the merits of the author, it becomes necessary to say every thing that may be considered essential on the merits of the work itself; independent of the praises which have been bestowed on it by different Arabic authors, who never mention it without expressing the utmost regard for it.

Though according to the Arabic title it is supposed to contain only the explanation of unknown alphabets, it gives beside a *key to the hieroglyphics*, and in the same chapter a curious *account of the different classes of the Egyptian priests, their initiation and sacrifices;* so that we may consider its contents under these three heads.

Although it is difficult to say how many of the eighty alphabets herein deciphered may have been really used by nations, or how many letters in every one alphabet may have been disfigured and misrepresented either by the want of sufficient information in our author himself, or by the ignorance and blunders of the copyists; yet it is not presumption to assert, that real truth lies at the bottom of most of them, and that those which were not alphabets for common writing, were used as ciphers amongst diffcrent Oriental nations. The proof of which is evident from the circumstance, that some among these alphabets are used even at this day amongst Turks, Arabs, and Persians, as a kind of secret cipher for writing, without being understood by the generality. The commonest habet called by the author of them is the alp the *tree* alphabet.

The first three *alphabets* of the first chapter, viz. the *Cufic*, *Maghrabin*, and *Numeral*, or Indian alphabet, are universally known.

Cufic inscriptions are found through the whole extent of the ancient empire of the Arabs, in *Arabia*, *Persia*, *Syria*, *Egypt*, *Sicily*, and *Spain*.

The *Maghrabin* or Andalusian alphabet is the common character used at this moment in *Morocco*, and throughout the northernmost part of Africa.

The *numeral* or Indian character is known to every *true Arab* or *Persian,* and to many *Europeans;* it is also known that in many of the Oriental languages, as well as in the Greek, alphabetical letters are used for numbers. The numerical signs, (called by us *Arabic,* and by the Arabs more properly *Indian* numbers) used *vice versa* for letters, form an alphabet, which is generally known, and particularly used in the *daftardám,* or *treasury office,* for accounts.

The seven alphabets contained in the second chapter merit the utmost attention from every Orientalist. The *Hebrew, Syrian* and *Greek* are already known to us; the *Nabathean* and *Masnad* or *Himyáric* we have heard of in history; but the *Lacam* and *Cerrebian* alphabets are unknown even by name.

The difference of the Hebrew, Syrian, an Greek letters from the usual alphabets o these languages may be, perhaps, mere mistakes of the copyist, but in spite of thi conjecture, 'they deserve the closest examina tion, for the author by birth a Caldean o

Nabathean, must have been well acquainted with the original form of these alphabets.

The *Himyáric* or *Masnad* alphabet is very often mentioned in Oriental and European books, but this is the first specimen which has appeared of it.*

Whether the *Barrabi* alphabet is the alphabet of the people called *Barrabars,* or whether the *Lacami* alphabet is originally an Abyssinian one, are questions difficult to decide.

The alphabets of the *third, fourth, fifth, sixth,* and *seventh* chapters, bearing the names of planets, constellations, philosophers, and kings may be considered as so many Oriental ciphers, which, at the time they were collected in this book, were, perhaps, named

---

* "As to the Himyáric letters, or those which are mentioned by the name of *Almasnad* we are still in total darkness, the traveller *Niebuhr* having been unfortunately prevented from visiting some ancient monuments in Yemen which are said to have inscriptions on them."

Sir William Jones's fourth anniversary Discourse.

after some celebrated men, to whom their invention was ascribed. The names themselves (as is commonly the case in all translations from a foreign language into Arabic) are so strangely altered and disfigured, that it was possible, but in very few cases, to guess the real meaning of them, and to translate them with the true original name.

The *Mimshim*, antidiluvian, or primeval alphabet deciphered in the last chapter, is highly interesting: for it shows the transition of the hieroglyphics from being signs expressive of words to the signification of simple letters; and the existence of *such* a hieroglyphical alphabet is sufficiently proved by the observations made on old Egyptian monuments; it shows, at the same time, the different modifications of the old Syrian and Caldean alphabets.

It is left to the reader to make the comparison between these characters and the known Oriental alphabets.

We proceed now to the hieroglyphics called

in Arabic *Hermesian alphabets,* from *Hermes,* who, according to Oriental history, was the first king of the ancient Egyptians. It is impossible to clear up entirely the darkness in which the history of this *triple Hermes* is involved. He is, however, evidently the *Hermes Trismegistus* of the Greeks, and possibly the same with the triple *Ráma* of the Indians.

The old kings of Egypt are comprehended by us under the general name of *Pharaohs.* The Oriental historians divide them into three dynasties, viz. 1. the *Hermesian:* 2. the *Pharaohs;* and 3. the *Coptic* or properly *Egyptian* kings. To the first, and particularly to *Hermes the threefold* himself, they ascribe the tombs, catacombs, temples, palaces, pyramids, obelisks, sphinxes, and all the royal, funeral, religious, and astronomical monuments, which astonish the traveller in Upper Egypt. But incapable of distinguishing them, or of finding out their true appropriation, they believe all of them to have been constructed for the purpose of hiding treasures, of raising spirits, of telling fortunes and future events, of performing chemical operations, of attracting affection, of repelling evils, or of indicating approaching enemies; and they call them, according to these supposed purposes, treasure chambers, conjuring buildings, astrological tables, alchemical monuments, magical spells, talismans, and magic alarm-posts.

The secrets of the contents of these monuments, or of the arts by means of which they are erected, were expressed, as they believe, by the hieroglyphics upon them, which being invented by *Hermes*, and kept secret by his descendants, were called the Hermesian alphabet.*

This specimen of Oriental writers being known to us, it is difficult either to confirm

---

* This idea of impervious secrecy is obvious in the expression come down to us of a thing being hermetically closed or sealed.

As there occurs in the course of the manuscript a great

TRANSLATOR'S PREFACE.

or to contradict the explanation of our author.

The most reasonable objections which can be made against the explanation of many of the hieroglyphics is counterbalanced by the evident truth, that a great many of them are known to have been invariably used in astronomy and chemistry for expressing the same objects; if the meaning of some of them does not prove satisfactory, there are others, to the truth of which no important objection

---

number of words relative to magical arts and charms, we submit here to the reader the translation of the principal ones:

Treasure chambers.
Conjuring buildings.
Astrological tables.
Alchemical monuments.
Magical spells.
Talismans.
Magic alarm-posts.
Inscriptions.
Secrets of the stars.
Conjuring spirits.
Fumigations.

Compounds; philtres.
Alchemistry.
The knowledge of spirits.
Planet-rings.
Magic black-art.
Magician.
Soothsayer.
Priest.
Pyramids.
Secrets, mysterious things.

can be made. Such are the hieroglyphics mentioned to have been represented on the tombs for conveying to posterity the character, mode of life, and death of the person buried therein. The seven figures (see hieroglyphics, original p. 124,) said to have been engraved on the tombs of men killed by violent death, show evidently the different modes of it: lightning, decollation, bite of a serpent, death by a hatchet, by poison, by a poniard, or by strangulation. The same concordance between the hieroglyphical sign, and the object meant, will be discovered by a close inspection of the four tables of hieroglyphics.

It will be sufficient to mention here a single instance of original merit, and a true discovery made by this manuscript, viz. the name of one of the most interesting hieroglyphics, which, after the explanation given by the author, is evidently what *Kircher* calls *anima mundi*, but the ancient name of which never has yet been explained. It is written *Bahámíd*, and translated into Arabic by the word *calf*.

TRANSLATOR'S PREFACE.

It is superfluous to recall here to the memory of the reader the great antiquity and mysterious sense of the idolatrous veneration in which this calf has been continually held. It is superfluous to repeat any thing that has been said on the worship of *Apis* in Egypt, renewed by the Israelites in the worship of the calf, and preserved at this moment in the mysterious rites of the Druses. Let us remember only a circumstance which shows wonderfully the concordance and relation of the name of *Bahûmíd* and its translation.

Bahumed or *Bahumet* is related in the History of the Templars to have been one of their secret and mysterious formulas, with which they addressed the idol of a *calf* in their secret assemblies. Different etymological explanations and descriptions of this word have been brought forward, but none surely so satisfactory as this, which proves that the Templars had some acquaintance with the hieroglyphics, probably acquired in Syria.

If, therefore, the explanation of the hieroglyphics given in this book deserves attention, the account of the four classes of Egyptian priests, their initiation, and sacrifices, is no less interesting.

In what a curious and new light do the catacombs of Sacara, containing the mummies of birds, appear by the account of those animals being embalmed at the initiation of the priests, wrapped up in a greater or lesser quantity of linen, and deposited in pits?

How evident does it become that the Judaic law of the first-born being offered to the Lord on the temple's threshold, is of Egyptian origin?

How interesting would it be to ascertain whether any of the thirty-two inscriptions seen by the author near Bagdad are actually to be found, or whether the shape of the letters of some pieces of poetry found by modern travellers in the neighbourhood of the ruins of Babylon, bear any resemblance to the *Chaldean, Nabathean, Sabean,* or *Curdic*

TRANSLATOR'S PREFACE.

alphabets? Certain it is that, though reason and fancy, truth and fable, may have contributed an equal share to the composition of this book, it must be considered notwithstanding as one of the most curious, the most interesting, and the most valuable manuscripts that have been found among the treasures of the East; and the translation, it is hoped, will be thought an acceptable gift to the curious and learned.

Having lately found in the bibliographical work of *Hadji Calfa*, and in another Encyclopedia, some notices about the author of this Treatise, and some other of his works, I have judged that a transcript of them, with a translation, would not be uninteresting in this place.

In the bibliographical and encyclopedial work of *Hadji Calfa*, entitled, كشف الظنون عن أسماً الكتب و الفنون i. e. *Elucidation of the Names of Books and Sciences*, we find under the article حكمت *Philosophy*, where the names of the most famous translators under the califs are enumerated, the following passage: وابن وحشيه نقل من النبطية الي العربية and IBN WAHSHIH *was employed in translating from the Nabathean into Arabic.*

In another encyclopedial work, the title of which is, كتاب الدر النظيم في احوال علوم التعليم, *The well-arranged Pearls of scientific Instruction,* we become acquainted with the titles of some other curious works translated by our author. Under the article علم كيميا is the following passage: ومن كتب القدما سدرة المنتهي نقل ابن وحشيه عن النبط *And among the oldest books upon this science is the Sidrat ul muntahí, (The Tree of Paradise) translated by* IBN WAHSHIH *from the Nabathean.*

In the same work under the head علم سيميا *Natural Magic,* (which they distinguish from سحر or *Supernatural Magic,)* we are told that Natural Magic is divided into two branches, the first treating of the knowledge of the particular properties of plants, metals, animals, &c.; and the second, of the composition and construction of artificial machines; after which the author says—و من الكتب المجبره في *Among the books written on the first branch is that entitled Taafinát, that is Putrifactions, translated from the Nabathean by* IBN WAHSHIH.

Finally under the head of علم فلاحة *Science of Agriculture,* as the most classical of all books is quoted الفلاحة النبطية نقل ابن وحشيه *The Agriculture of the Nabatheans, a translation of* IBN WAHSHIH. A copy of this work, if I am not mistaken, may be found in the Bodleian Library at Oxford. See also Herbelot under the word *Falahat.*

Since writing the above, I have discovered that this rare book was not unknown to Kircher, who in his work on the Hieroglyphics, under the first paragraph, *Occasio hujus operis,* says: " Quatuor lustra jam prope eguntur— " quo—Romam ut in obeliscis Romanis spe-

"cimen quoddam exhiberem hieroglyphicæ
"interpretationis, e Gallia vocor, cujus lit-
"teraturæ hucusque incognitæ ex pervetusto
"*Arabico codice* instaurationem me moliri
"fama ferebatur."

And farther below in the same *epistola parænetica* talking of his means, and naming different authors, he concludes the enumeration by saying; "quos inter principem sanè "locum obtinet *Aben Vaschia.*" Then again page 109 in the text naming his Arabic authors— "*Gelaledden, Aben Regel, et Aben* "*Vahschia* de culturâ Ægyptiorum, et libro "de antiquitatæ vitæ, moribus, litteris vete- "rum Ægyptiorum, quos penes me habeo, "ex quibus haud exiguum ad Hieroglyphi- "cum institutionem subsidium allatum est."
And then: "Nam *Aben Wahschia*—primus "Ægyptios libros in linguam Arabicam trans- "tulit, quem nos Melitæ inter spolia Tur- "corum repostum singulari Dei providentiâ "arabicum reperimus."

Now though these quotations shew that the

TRANSLATOR'S PREFACE.

manuscript was not, as I supposed, unknown, yet they enhance the value of it by the worth attached to it by a man like Kircher. The same work is now I believe at Paris, where there has lately been a great talk of the manuscript alphabets at the imperial library transported from *Rome;* which renders the publishing of it in England the more interesting. Kircher found his copy at Malta amongst the Turks, and I this at Cairo amongst the Arabs.

The author mentions his having deposited this work in the treasury of *Abdolmelic* in the year 214. Now the Calif just named reigned in the middle of the first century of the Hejira, and unless there was a public establishment of treasury or library founded by that Calif, and still bearing his name, wherein *Ibn Wahshih* may have deposited it in the year 214, long after the death of the Calif, it is impossible to reconcile those dates, particularly as all my endeavours to find anywhere else the time wherein *Ibn Wahshih* lived, have proved fruitless.

TRANSLATOR'S PREFACE.

The following Table shewing the power of the Arabic letters in Roman character will be useful to those who may not be acquainted with them.

ا *alif* has the power of A.
ب *bá*   ditto   B.
ت *tá*   ditto   T.
ث *sá*   ditto   S, by some pronounced like *th* in the English word *think*.
ج *jim* has the power of J, English.
ح *há*   ditto   H, very much aspirated.
خ *khá*   ditto   KH, a guttural sound like the German c
د *dál*   ditto   D.
ذ *zál*   ditto   Z, by some pronounced like *th* in the English word *those*.
ر *rá*   ditto   R.
ز *zá*   ditto   Z.
س *sin*   ditto   S.
ش *shin* ditto   SH, English.
ص *sád*   ditto   S, with a strong effort from the throat
ض *zád*   ditto   Z, with a strong effort from the throat, by some pronounced like a *d* with a guttural sound.

TRANSLATOR'S PREFACE.

غ *ghayn*	has	the power of GH, or rather the Northumbrian R.
ف *fá*	ditto	F.
ق *káf*	ditto	K, very hard.
ك & ک *káf*	ditto	K.
ل *lám*	ditto	L.
م *mím*	ditto	M.
ن *nún*	ditto	N.
و *wáw*	ditto	W and ú.
ه *há*	ditto	H soft.
ي *yá*	ditto	Y and í.

AN
EXPLANATION
OF
ANCIENT ALPHABETS AND HIEROGLYPHICS,
&c. &c.

THE
AUTHOR'S PREFACE.

Praise to God, and health to his servants, who have pure hearts. Amen! My object is to collect the rudiments of alphabets used by antient nations, doctors and learned philosophers in their books of science, for the use of the curious and studious, who apply themselves to philosophical and mystic sciences.

Each alphabet is represented in its old shape and form, the original name of it recorded, and the power of the characters written underneath with red ink* in Arabic letters, to the end that they may be better distinguished.

I have arranged the work in chapters, and entitled it, *The long desired Knowledge of occult Alphabets attained.* With the aid of God!

---

* This distinction, for obvious reasons, has not been imitated in the printed copy.

AN EXPLANATION
OF
ANCIENT ALPHABETS AND HIEROGLYPHICS, &c.

CHAPTER I.

The three usual (Oriental) alphabets, viz: the Cufic, *the* Maghrabin, *and the* Indian.

SECTION I. The *Cufic* alphabet. Our Lord Ismael (peace be with him!) was the first who spoke Arabic, and who wrote the Cufic, of which nine different sorts were used. The ground of all of them is the Cufic alphabet, known by the name of *Sûrí*. (See page 4 of the Arabic text beginning from the right.)

SECTION II. The *Maghrabin* (western) or *Andalusian* alphabet, (v. orig. p. 5.)

SECTION III. The *Indian* alphabet of three different sorts, (v. orig. p. 6, 7, 8.)

CHAPTER II.

The seven most celebrated old alphabets.

SECTION I. The *Syrian* alphabet, (v. orig. p. 9.)

SECTION II. The old *Nabathean* alphabet, (v. orig. p. 10.)

SECTION III. The *Hebrew* alphabet, (v. orig. p. 11.)

SECTION IV. The *Berrabian* alphabet, (v. orig. p. 12.)

SECTION V. The *Lukumian* alphabet, (v. orig. p. 13.)

SECTION VI. The *Musnad* or (*Hamyaritic*) alphabet, (v. orig. p. 14.)

SECTION VII. The Greek alphabet, commonly called the alphabet of the philosophers, (v. orig. p. 15.)

CHAPTER III.

The particular Alphabets (or rather Cyphers) of the seven most celebrated Philosophers.

SECTION I. The alphabet of *Hermes*, (v. orig. p. 16.)

Section II. The alphabet of *Cleomenes*, (v. orig. p. 17.)

Section III. The alphabet of *Plato*, (v. orig. p. 18.)

Section. IV. The alphabet of *Pythagoras*, (v. orig. p. 19.)

Section V. The alphabet of *Scalinus*, (v. orig. p. 20.)

Section VI. The alphabet of *Socrates*, (v. orig. p. 21.)

Section VII. The alphabet of *Aristotle*, (v. orig. p. 22.)

CHAPTER IV.

The four-and-twenty Alphabets, (or rather Cyphers,) that were used after the seven preceding, by the most celebrated Philosophers and learned Men.

Section I. The alphabet of *Belinos*, the philosopher, (v. orig. p. 23.)

Section II. Another *Berrabian* alphabet invented by the philosopher *Soorid*, (v. orig. p. 24.)

Section III. The alphabet of the philosopher, *Pherentius*, who wrote therewith his philosophical books, (v. orig. p. 25.)

SECTION IV. The *Moallak*, or suspended alphabet, invented by *Ptolomy* the Greek, (v. orig. p. 26.)

SECTION V. The *Marboot* or connected alphabet, invented by *Marconos?* the philosopher. He wrote therewith books on *talismans*, (v. orig. p. 27.)

SECTION VI. The *Giorgian* alphabet, invented by philosopher *Marjanòs*, (v. orig. p. 28.)

SECTION VII. The old *Nabathean* alphabet, (v. orig. p. 29.)

SECTION VIII. The red alphabet, invented and used by the philosopher *Magnis*, (v. orig. p. 30.)

SECTION IX. The *Talisman* alphabet, invented by the Greek philosopher *Ghámígháshír?* (v. orig. p. 31.)

SECTION X. The mysterious alphabet, invented by *Heliaosh?* the Greek philosopher, who used it in his books, (v. orig. p. 32)

SECTION XI. The alphabet of *Costoodjis* the Greek philosopher. He wrote in this alphabet, three hundred and sixty books on divinity, talismans, astrology, magic, influence of planets and fixed stars, and on the conjuration of spirits, (v. orig. p. 33.)

SECTION XII. The alphabet of *Hermes Abootat*

the philosopher. He wrote on the noble art (of philosophical secrets.) He constructed in upper Egypt treasure chambers, and set up stones containing magic inscriptions, which he locked, and guarded by the charm of this alphabet, extracted from the regions of darkness, (v. orig. p. 34.)

SECTION XIII. The alphabet of *Colphotorios* the philosopher. He was deeply learned in the knowledge of spirits and cabalistic spells, in talismans, astrological aspects, and in the magic and black art. Philosophers and learned men have used this alphabet in their books and writings in preference to others, on account of its different extraordinary qualities, (v. orig. p. 35.)

SECTION XIV. The alphabet of *Syourianos* the philosopher, (v. orig. p. 36.) He wrote in this alphabet on astronomy, and the secrets of the stars; on talismans, and their qualities; on magic alarm-posts; on the effects of planet-rings; and on the invocation and conjuration of spirits.

SECTION XV. The alphabet of *Philaos* the philosopher, (v. orig. p. 37.) He invented miraculous fumigations, marvellous compounds, talismans, and astrological tables. He constructed the treasure-chambers in the pyramids, and guarded them with the charm of wonderful alarm-posts,

Section XVI. The alphabet of *Dioscoride* the philosopher, commonly called the Tree al phabet, (v. orig. p. 38.). He wrote on trees shrubs, and herbs, and of their secret, useful, an noxious qualities in this alphabet, used since i their books by different philosophers.

Section XVII. The *Davidian* alphabet, (v orig. p. 38.) This alphabet was particularly use in India, and by many learned men in their writ ings on medicine, philosophy, and politics. I is one of the most celebrated alphabets.

Section XVIII. The alphabet of *Democrate* the philosopher, (v. orig. p. 40.) The Gree philosophers delighted very much in this alpha bet, making use of it for the secrets and mysterie of their wisdom. They believed it to be the sam with the Mercurial alphabet extracted from th regions of darkness.

Section XIX. The alphabet of the *Cophti Egyptian* philosophers, (v. orig. p. 41.) In thi they noted their calculations and indications, an wrote the inscriptions on their treasuries, and th secrets of divinity. *Kophtrim*, one of Noah's de scendants, invented this alphabet. It is even no used in calculation.

Section XX. The *Farganian* alphabet, (

orig. p. 42.) It was invented by seven Rom[an]
philosophers, who wrote a great number of boo[ks]
on chymistry, magic, and medicine. Their pri[n]
cipal was *Diojánes*, the great Roman king. Th[e]
alphabet was much celebrated in his time, but
now forgotten.

SECTION XXI. The alphabet of *Zosimus*,
Jew philosopher, (v. orig. p. 43.) This alphab[et]
was very much refined by the Hebrew philos[o]
phers, who made use of it for writing their ho[ly]
books deposited in Jerusalem.

SECTION XXII. The alphabet of *Marshol* th[e]
philosopher, (v. orig. p. 44.) He was a wise a[nd]
learned man, who wrote on different arts a[nd]
sciences.

SECTION XXIII. The alphabet of *Arcadjir*
the Greek philosopher, (v. orig. p. 45.) He i[n]
vented a great number of wonderful compound
fumigations, royal theriacs, medicines, and effe[c]
tual remedies.

SECTION XXIV. The alphabet of *Plato* t[he]
Greek philosopher, (v. orig. p. 46.) It is sa[id]
that each letter of this alphabet had different i[m]
ports, according to the affair and thing treat[ed]
of.

F

CHAPTER V.

The Alphabets of the Seven Planets.

Section I. The alphabet of *Saturn*, (v. orig p. 47.)

Section II. The alphabet of *Jupiter*, (v. orig p. 48.)

Section III. The alphabet of *Mars*, or philosopher *Behram*, (v. orig. p. 49.)

Section IV. The alphabet of the sun, th lord of heaven, (v. orig. p. 50.)

Section V. The alphabet of *Venus, Anaiti*, the celestial dancer, (v. orig. p. 51.)

Section VI. The alphabet of *Mercury* o *Hermes*, the secretary of heaven, (v. orig. p. 52.)

Section VII. The alphabet of the moo (v. orig. p. 53.)

CHAPTER VI.

The Alphabets of the Twelve Constellations.

Section I. The alphabet of *Aries*, under t influence of *Mars*, (v. orig. p. 54.)

Section II The alphabet of *Taurus*, under the influence of *Venus*, (v. orig. p. 55.)

Section III. The alphabet of the *Gemini*, under the influence of *Mercury*, (v. orig. p. 66.)

Section IV. The alphabet of *Cancer*, under the influence of the *Moon*, (v. orig. p. 57.)

Section V. The alphabet of *Leo*, under the influence of the *Sun*, (v. orig. p. 58.)

Section VI. The alphabet of the *Virgin*, influenced by *Mercury*, (v. orig. p. 59.)

Section VII. The alphabet of *Libra*, (v. orig. p. 60.)

Section. VIII. The alphabet of *Scorpio*, (v. orig. p. 61.) This alphabet was very much used by the Chaldeans in their impressions on hidden treasures, and in their books and writings concerning the secret influence of the planet Mars. This alphabet was transmitted by spiritual inspiration through *Marshimine* to the soothsayer *Arbiasios*, the *Nabathean*.

Section IX. The alphabet of *Sagittarius*, influenced by *Jupiter*, (v. orig. p. 62.)

Section X. The alphabet of *Capricorn* under the influence of *Saturn*, (v. orig. p. 63.) This alphabet was particularly appropriated to the use of the Babylonian and Persian philosophers, who kept it as a great secret. It was discovered after their extinction in their books, carried away by the Greeks. The Egyptian philosophers used it afterwards in their astronomical works.

SECTION XI. The alphabet of the sign *Aquarius,* under the influence of *Saturn,* (v. orig. p. 64.) It was particularly used by the Chaldeans and Sabeans in their incantation books, and also in their inscriptions relative to the science of spirits.

SECTION. XII. The alphabet of *Pisces,* (v. orig. p. 65.)

CHAPTER VII.

Alphabets of ancient Kings, viz: the Kings of Syria, *the* Hermesian *Kings of Egypt, the* Pharaohs, *the* Canaanites, Curds, Casdanians, Persians *and* Cophts.

SECTION I. The alphabet of king *Berdois* the Syrian, (v. orig. p. 68.) In this alphabet he wrote all his books on the minutiæ of divinity, and natural law.

SECTION II. The alphabet of king *Resiut,* the Egyptian Pharaoh, (v. orig. p. 69.) He constructed wonderful talismans and magical alarm-posts. All of them in this ancient alphabet.

SECTION III. The alphabèt of king *Kimas* the *Hermesian,* (v. orig. p. 70.) He wrote two hundred books on astronomy, on the secrets of physic, and on the qualities of plants and minerals.

SECTION IV. The alphabet of king *Mehrarish,* (v. orig. p. 71.) He was a famous soothsayer, deeply experienced in philosophy and divinity. He wrote more than a thousand books on other sciences.

SECTION V. The alphabet of king *Taberinos* the soothsayer, (v. orig. p. 72.) One of the alpha bets used by the Pharaohs in their inscriptions.

SECTION VI. The alphabet of king *Diosmos,* the Egyptian, (v. orig. p. 73.) He was one of the Pharaohs most renowned for magic, talismans, and astrological tables.

SECTION VII. The alphabet of king *Berhemio* the Egyptian, (v. orig. p. 74.) This is one of th oldest alphabets used by the magicians and Pha raohs in Egypt; and it was transferred from thes to the soothsayers of India and China.

SECTION VIII. The alphabet of king *Saaa* the soothsayer, (v. orig. p. 75.) He was one of th seven magicians, who were at the same time kings doctors, soothsayers, magicians, and philosophers who governed and cultivated Egypt, and built the great towns subsisting till this day.

SECTION IX. The alphabet of king *Belbeis*,* (v. orig. p. 76.) He built a town four *farsangs* long, full of admirable works, and wrote a great number of books in this alphabet.

SECTION X. The alphabet of king *Cophtrim*, the Egyptian, (v. orig. p. 77.) He was a great master in the art of constructing talismans and admirable alarm-posts, treasure spells, and wonderful images. He wrote an Encyclopedia of all sciences in this alphabet.

CHAPTER VIII.

The Alphabets called Hermesian, *viz. of the Disciples of* Hermes, *or the first dynasty of the Kings in* Egypt, *as we find them in the Writings of the Ancients.*

Every one of these kings invented, according

---

* He was perhaps the founder of an old Egyptian town, near *Belbeis*, the ruins of which have been found by the French. See the first Volume of the Décade Egyptienne.

to his own genius and understanding, a particular alphabet, in order that none should know them but the sons of wisdom. Few, therefore, are found who understand them in our time. They took the figures of different instruments, trees, plants, quadrupeds, birds, or their parts, and of planets, and fixed stars. In this manner these hieroglyphical alphabets became innumerable, like the alphabets of the Indians and Chinese. They were not arranged at all in the order of our letters *a, b, c, d,* but they had proper characters agreed upon by the inventors of these alphabets, and which differed in their figure and order, viz. they expressed water by ∿∿ They understood the secrets of nature, and endeavoured to express every thing by an appropriate sign, so that they might express it by its appearance.

Others followed the simple rules of geometry, deriving one alphabet from another, as the *Coofic* has been derived from the *Syrian,* the *Hebrew* from the *Chaldean,* the *Latin* from the *Greek,* and others, in this manner, from some original. Whosoever wishes to become acquainted with all the nice points of the knowledge of alphabets, may inquire for the book entitled *Solution of Secrets and Key of Treasures by Jaber Hayan Essoofi,* who enters into all the necessary explanations and details of this art. Our object is only to mention the most celebrated of these alphabets of the Hermesians, (or hieroglyphics,) and to indicate their particular qualities; for nobody is capable of giving a satisfactory explanation of them all.

God directs all things for the best.

SECTION I. Alphabet of the philosopher *Hermes* the great.

This alphabet is used on the *Obelisks*, the *Pyramids*, the *inscription tables* and *stones;* the *temples*, and other old buildings, from the time of the first *Pharaohs*. It does not consist in a series of letters like other alphabets, but in expressions composed according to the arrangement made by Hermes the great. These expressions consist in innumerable figures and signs, which are to lead the mind directly, and immediately to the object expressed thereby, viz: there is a sign which signifies the name of God Almighty, simply and alone. If they wished to express one of the particular attributes of God they added something to the original sign, and proceded in this manner, as you will perceive by the alphabet in question.

It is divided into three series, beside the celestial or supernatural objects. Let us begin with the

[17]

celestial objects, and the figures by which they were expressed in the *Hermesian language* represented as we have found them.

[18]

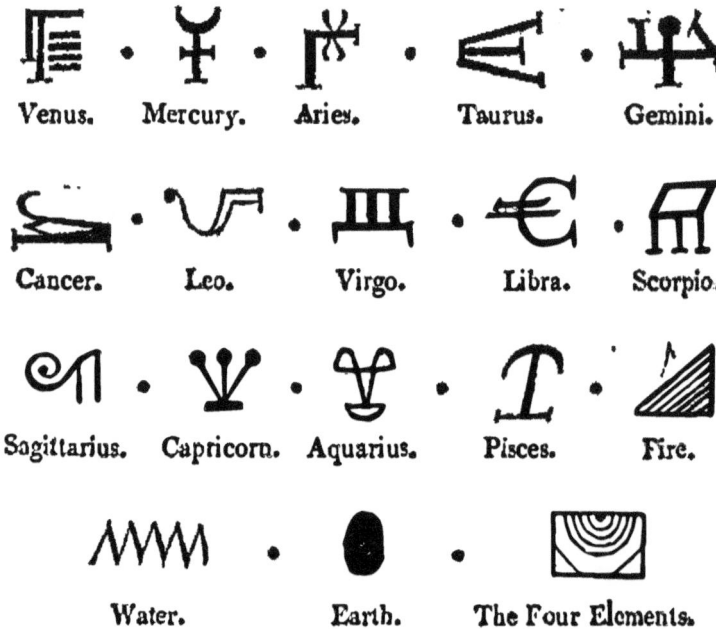

These are the figures of such of the celestial hieroglyphics, as we have been able to find and make out; and now we are going to represent the three other classes, according to promise, with all the different figures of the Hermesian alphabets, or hieroglyphics.

THE FIRST SERIES.

Hieroglyphics to express Words relative to Animal Actions and Affections.

[21]

[22]

Eloquence.	Opposition.	Falsehood.	Secrets of Nature.
Casualties.	Spiritual Secrets.	Art.	Weight.
Astronomy.	Talismans.	Magic.	Art of raising and conjuring Spirits.

This figure is expressive of the most sublime

secret, called originally *Bahumed* and *Kharuf* (or call), viz. *The Secret of the nature of the world*, or *The Secret of Secrets*, or *The Beginning and Return of every thing*.

To speak at length of this figure, is more than the limits of this book allow. We refer the curious, who wish for more explanation, to a book, which we have translated from our *Nabathean* language into *Arabic*, and entitled: *Sun of Suns and Moon of Moons*, illuminating the discovery of the *Hermesian* alphabets, or *hieroglyphics*, where he will be completely satisfied.

The *Hermesians* let nobody into the secrets of their knowledge but their disciples, lest the arts and sciences should be debased by being common amongst the vulgar. They hid therefore their secrets and treasures from them by the means of this alphabet, and by inscriptions, which could be read by nobody except the sons of wisdom and learning.

These initiated scholars were divided into four classes. The *first Class* comprehended the sect of the *Harámisah Alhawmiyah*, who were all descendants of *Hermes* the Great. They married daughters of their own race only, and never were allowed to have any kind of intercouse with strangers. No man in the world was acquainted with any of their secrets: they alone possessed them. They were the authors of the books commonly called the books of *Edris* (Enoch). They constructed temples dedicated to spirits, and buildings of magical wisdom. The few of those, who in our time are acquainted with this knowledge, live retired in some islands near the frontiers of *China*, and continue to tread the steps of their forefathers.*

The second class of the Hermesians, called *Harámisah Alpináwalúziyah*, the sons of the brother of Hermes, whose name was *Asclibianos*. They married within their own families only, and far from giving their countrymen any kind of trouble, they became necessary to them in all their business. The difference between them and the former consisted in the use of perfumes allowed to them, and in the liberty they enjoyed to see their relations at the entrance of the sun into the several signs of the zodiac, and at the commencement of each season. On the latter occasion they had a feast of seven days. The *Alhawmiy'ah*, on the contrary, were

* Perhaps the *Brahmans* may be here alluded to as the followers of the Hermesian philosophy. On the intercourse between India, Egypt, and China, see Sir William Jones's Annual Discourses in the Asiatic Researches.

continually occupied with reading the holy books, with acts of devotion, and with fasting. They had only one feast in the year, lasting eight and twenty days *(a month)*, beginning at the entrance of the sun into the sign Aries. At this time they approached their relations, and enjoyed perfumes and other pleasures of life. They confessed the unity of God the Creator of all things. Blessed be his Name!

They never communicated their secrets, and Hermetic treasures to any body, but they preserved them from generation to generation, till our days.

When a child was born to them, the mother took it to the priest of the temple, where trial of the children used to be made. She laid it down on the threshold of the temple without speaking a word. The priest then came with a golden cup full of water in his hands, accompanied by six other priests. He said prayers, and sprinkled water over the child. If it moved, and turned its face towards the threshold, the priest took it by the hand, and conducted it into the interior of the temple, where there was a coffin prepared on purpose. There they said prayers and performed ceremonies for an hour. Then the priest covered the face of the child with a silk handkerchief; a green one for girls, and a red one for boys; put it in the coffin, shut it up, and took in his hand a stick with three heads made of silver, and set with jewels and precious stones.

The father, mother, and relations of the child entered at this moment, and performed prayers and hymns in humble devotion. The priest then struck the coffin with his staff thrice, and cried out: " In the name of the Lord thy God who " created and made thee, exist by his wisdom, " speak out the inmost secrets of the events of thy " life! Amen, Amen, for ever and ever!" The whole assembly performed seven adorations, and then stood up. The child said, " Health and " heaven's blessing to thee!" The priest returned his greetings, and said " What is thy name? In " what consists thy sacrifice, and what means of " subsistence dost thou desire? At what hour hast " thou been adorned with this noble body, and these " gracious features, (i. e. when wert thou born?) " Art thou to remain here as thy brethren, or art " thou merely a travelling guest? I ask thee in " the name of God, the all-vivifying, the un- " changeable, the eternal One, without end or " beginning, in whose power are all things visible " and invisible, the Lord of heaven and earth, the "most High and supreme Being; and I conjure thee to answer and promise, that as long as thou shalt exist in this world, thou wilt never reveal our secrets to any stranger."

The child promised it in the name of truth, which is written on the table existing from the beginning of things, in the table of Fate preserved in heaven. The child was then told, that he was received amongst the number of the wise and learned, the sons of science; or amongst the masters of mechanical arts and works. They conversed with him on every subject. They put him different questions, and heard his answers. A priest standing by noted the answers on a table of stone, and hung it up in the temple.

After this, they called the child, opened the coffin, purified it with fumigations, and performed a sacrifice consisting of a quadruped, or a bird. They burnt the blood shed, purified the body, and wrapt it up in a piece of fine white linen an hundred and twenty fold for a male, and sixty for a female. They put it into a pot of earth, and deposited it in the pit of sacrifices. All this was performed according to secret rites known to nobody but themselves.

The coffin mentioned was made in the shape of

a little chest, of the length of the child, made of olive wood, and adorned with gold and precious stones. If the child happened afterwards to mention this mysterious reception, they rejected it, saying, " This child cannot be trusted with our " secrets and mysteries, for it may betray them." They afterwards brought forward some fault on which they grounded their exclusion. If the initiated person had already grown up, and wished to withdraw from their order, he was sure to die within three days.

One of their greatest secrets was involved in the sacrifice of their great feast. They took seven bulls and seven rams, and fed them with certain herbs, called *Hashishat uz Zohrah* and *Tájulmalik* and in their language *Shikrek*, during seven days, and gave them purified water to drink. The seventh day of the week they decked them out with gold and jewels, and bound them in golden chains. The priests sung prayers, hymns, and psalms in the great temple. The people arranged in their different classes, worshipped God. The chief of the sacrificers advanced then, and made with the triple staff a sign to the bulls and rams, which, without any other action or impulse, were thereby delivered from their chains, advanced, and voluntarily stretched out their necks towards the sacrificer, who immolated them. The heads of the victims were put in the coffin, and the rest of their bodies embalmed with different kinds of drugs, as aloes, amber, musk, camphor, and storox, and the great prayer began.

Every priest appeared in the dress of his class, reading the holy books. They prostrated themselves to the earth, remaining thus for a whole hour, and after they had raised their heads, the first of the sacrificers began to speak on all the events to be divined from this. He was followed by the second and third, and so on till the last. One of the priests wrote down every speech, the results of which they compared.

As they practised different rites, the real import and meaning of which nobody could tell but themselves; and all this proves sufficiently the great care with which they kept their secrets hidden. They said, " These things are come down from our father *Adam*, *Seth*, and *Hermes*, or *Edris (Enoch)*, the triple." There were sundry other particulars worthy to be mentioned; but we will not exceed the bounds of our expressed purpose.

The third class was called *Ashrákiyún* (Eastern), or the children of the sister of Hermes, who is known amongst the Greek by the name of *Trismegistos Thoosdios*. This class was intermixed with some strangers and profane, who found means to get hold of the expressions of their hearts. Their sciences and knowledge are come down to us.

The fourth class, denominated *Masháwun*, (*walkers, or peripatetic philosophers*), was formed by the strangers, who found means to mingle with the children and family of *Hermes*. They were the first who introduced the worship of the stars and constellations, and who forsook the worship of the God of Gods. (Be his glory exalted—there is no other God but him!) From hence came their divisions, and every thing that has been handed down to us, proceeds originally from these two sects, the *Ashrákiyún*, eastern, and *Masháwun*, peripatetic philosophers.

Learn then, O reader! the secrets, mysteries, and treasures of the *Hieroglyphics*, not to be found, and not to be discovered any where else. Formerly a knowledge of them could not be acquired but by immense pains and expense, by a great number of years, and a long course of travels, and now lo! these treasures are laid open for thy enjoyment. Take possession of them, keep and guard them with the utmost care and secrecy. Profoundly learned philosophers and curious students only have attained this knowledge. Let us now proceed to explain the hieroglyphics promised above.

SECOND SERIES.

Hieroglyphics significant of Words relating to Trees and Plants, and their Produce.

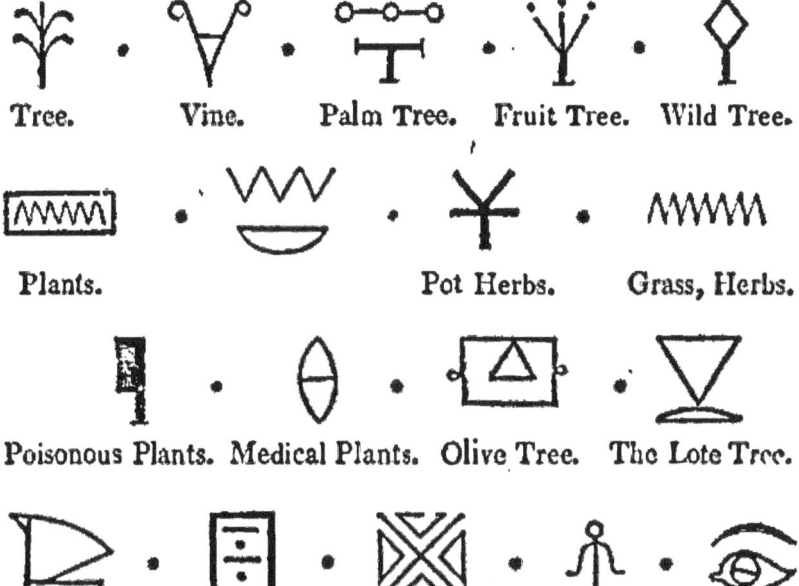

[32]

[34]

Apple. Kasfarat. A. Sesame. Citron. Honey.

Sabar. A. Myrrh. Safron. Gum Sandres. Mámisá. A.

Gum. Mulberry. Fig. Indian Spikenard. Pruin, Plum.

Storax. Frankincense. Civet. Musk. Amber.

Laudanum. Pitch. Naptha. Manna. Hasak. A.

Múmiyá, viz. the drugs used for embalming. Sweet Marjoram. ? Ghárikún. A.

Rue. ? Onion. Linseed. Cotton.

Now we have to mention, if it pleases God, the hieroglyphical figures for minerals, or *the Third Series of Hieroglyphics*.

The philosopher *Dúshám* mentions these signs in his book on *the qualities of planets and minerals*. He used this alphabet to design their secret qualities. Learn it, and keep it well, O reader, for it is one of the profoundest secrets.

THE FOURTH SERIES.

Hieroglyphics expressive of Words and Ideas belonging to Minerals.

[37]

[38]

White Clay.　　Rahaj-ásfar. A.　　Glass.　　Hajar Jabasín. A.

A Species of Green Stone.　Sulphur.　Sakhar. A.　A Yellow Stone.

Khamáhán. A.　A Kind of Emerald.　Agate.　A Green Stone.

Adamantine Spar.　Sawán. A.　Sházanah. A.　Serpent Stone.

Bitumen.　　Diamond.　　A Censer.　　Iron chain.

A Transparent Stone.　Cutting of Stones.　Solution of Stones.　Trituration of Stones.

Engraving of Stones.　Hajar-us-sabaj. A.　A Kind of Shell.　A Snail Shell.　Hajar Hindí. A.

[39]

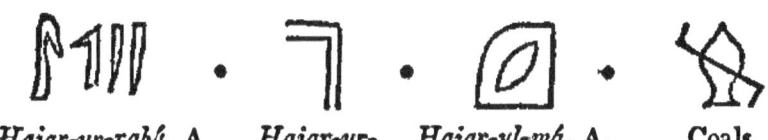

 .  .

Hajar-ur-rahá. A.　　Hajar-ur-　　Hajar-ul-má. A.　　Coals.
　　　　　　　　　　rakhwa. A.

 .  .

Crucible.　　Artificial Well.　　Khársíní. A.　　Fixed Quicksilver.

 .  .  .

Trituration of Stones.　　Composition of Stones.　　Marble Stone.

 . .  .

Calcination of Stones.　　Bezoar.　　Silver Magnet.　　Blood Stone.

 .  . .

Hajar-ul-Khattáf. A.　　Rain Stone.　　Rock Salt.　　Naptha Stone.
　　　　　　　　　　　Hail?

 . 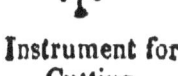 .  .

Kaisúr. A.　　Hajar samáwí. A.　　Serpentine Stone.　　Collyrium.

Asmad. A.　　Instrument for　　Breaking and　　A Pestle and
　　　　　　　Cutting.　　　　Cleaving.　　　Mortar.

Kitabat-ul-Hajar. A.   Water springing from the Rock.   Hercometry particularly applied to Stone.

And here end the figures of the *hieroglyphics*, which we have found, and can make out.

We have mentioned only those we are certain of, but these we know to be exact and right. Perhaps every one of these figures may have had more than one signification, according to the different classes of priests, who wishing to hide their secrets one from the other, gave their signs different meanings.

God is the leader to the best.

APPENDIX.

Antidiluvian Alphabets preserved by the Nabatheans, Chaldeans, and Sabeans.

THE first called the *Shishim alphabet*, was used for writing sentences of wisdom on clay, which being burnt became pottery (v. orig. p. 114.)

The following alphabet was also used by the Pharaohs, who convinced of its being an antidiluvian one, used to write with it the books of prayer and liturgies, which they used in their temples before their gods.

I have myself seen in Upper Egypt, inscription tables and stones engraved with this alphabet. The Pharaohs firmly believed in its antiquity, and the Nabatheans and Chaldeans continued in the same opinion (v. orig. p. 115.)

The original alphabets, from which all other ancient and modern ones have been derived, are no more than three.

1. The *old Syrian alphabet*, or the first original divine alphabet, taught by God the Almighty to Adam.

2. The *Celestial alphabet*, or the alphabet in which the books which Seth (health be with him) received from heaven were written.

3 The *alphabet of Enoch* brought down by the angel Gabriel.

This opinion is generally received and agreed upon by different nations and sects.

Chanukha has confirmed the truth in his books. *Agathodaimon* is of the same opinion in his book *on secret things.* He says, that all divine (inspired) legislators have preserved their secrets in one of these three alphabets. The indication of this great man was our guide, we have collected and copied these alphabets, according to his opinions and belief. Pay attention, in order that thou mayst walk in the right path.

The *Syrian* alphabet had, according to the opinion of the most learned men, the following characters (v. orig. p. 117).

These, however, were the figures of the letters in the earliest ages, which were changed by time, as you may perceive (v. orig. p. 118).

This is the alphabet in which Adam (peace be

with him) wrote his books. Who says the contrary says falsehood, and God knows the best.

On the Shimshim Alphabet.

It was inspired by divine revelation, and varied in four different manners by the people who used it, viz. the *Hermesians*, the *Nabatheans*, the *Sabeans*, and *Chaldeans*. These are the four most ancient people, from whom all modern nations have derived their writing.

The characters of the *Hermesians*, with the particular names and powers of their letters.

Character.	Name.	Power.
	Ayhúm	A.
	Yawúk	I or Y.
	Kā-a	K *hard*.
	Ghúwá	Gh.
	Bídam	B.

Character.	Name.	Power.
	Kághach	K soft.
	Rún	R.
	Jahúm	J English.
	Shá	Sh ditto
	Danaz	D.
	Máyib	M.
	Tanras	T.
	Hin	H soft.
		N.
	Thanad	Th in Think.
	Wú Awd	W, U.

Character.	Name.	Power.
	Saparam	S.
	Khayúrí	Kh.
	Zid	Z.
	Lúghaf	L.
	Aay	(ع) A.
	Zayúm	(ظ) Z.
	Sikám	(ص) .
	Zalap	Z.
	Takar	(ط) T.
	Hisat	H *hard.*
	Fisat	F.

Character.	Name.	Power.
	Zanaz	(ض) Z.
	Chil	Ch English.
	Kam	A kind of hard K.
	Nayím	A kind of N.
	Pap.	P.
	Kál	A kind of K.
	Zayimap	A kind of Z.
	Hám	A sort of soft H.
	Japlat	A kind of J English.
	Jasaz.	A kind of compound of C
	Jáyigh.	J French.

Many of these letters are not used either in Arabic or Persian, except by those who have the knowledge of this language. They are arranged in a contrary order to that commonly received of A, B, C. The order in which they are disposed, is founded on the nature of their language. Understand this, that thou mayst go the right way.

The Nabatheans gave the preference to the figures of animals, disposed according to their natural order, and each of these figures had its secret signification, viz.

If they wished to express a powerful, brave, cunning, and avaricious king, they painted the figure of a man with the head of a lion, pointing with one of his fingers to a fox before him. If they wished to express the attribute of understanding, sagacity, and wisdom, they represented a man with the head of an elephant, pointing with one of his fingers to a sitting ape. If they wished to give him the attributes of justice, generosity, and liberality, they drew a man with a bird's head, and before him a balance, a sun, and a moon. If they meant to represent him cruel, faithless, and ignorant they gave him a dog's, ass's, or boar's head, with a pot of fire, and a sword before him.

A sick, weak, and decrepid man was represented

by the figure of a man, followed by the figures  and before him the figure of Saturn, sometimes with the figures

A man killed by violent death, was represented by the figure of a man with the head of an owl, or a bat, and behind him a scorpion with the character ⩩ and the figure of the devil behind him, with these characters ⸻ .

If he was poisoned, he was represented with a crab's, or beetle's head, and a glass, or bowl, before him, and the characters ⸻ .

Death occasioned by plague, a hot fever, or corruption of the blood and the humours, was represented by a man sitting in a chair, with an arrow in his hand and over his head a   upon the back of the chair, and before him the figures

Honours, authority, and a comfortable situation, were designed by a man holding in his hand a ball, or circle, upon his head a crown, before him a raven, and behind him a dog, with these characters in a circle round them

A man of perfect wisdom and understanding, accomplished in all his ways, and without the least blame, was painted with a beautiful face, with wings like an angel, holding in his hands a hook, in which he looked, a sword and a balance, and behind him two vases, one of them full of water, and the other of blazing fire. Under his right foot a ball, with a crab painted on it, and under his left a deep pot full of serpents, scorpions, and different reptiles, the covering of which had the shape of an eagle's head.

See, my son! these are the secrets of these people, with which nobody was acquainted but themselves. I have seen, in one of the hieroglyphical buildings in Upper Egypt, the representation I am going to describe.

This building was a temple of the Lord *Adonai,* whom sun and moon serve. It represented a coffin, adorned with curious figures and admirable ornaments. A vine growing, with its leaves spread over it. The Lord (God) was standing upon the coffin, with a staff in his hand, out of the end of which a tree shot forth and overshadowed it.

Behind the coffin was seen a pit full of blazing fire, and four angels catching serpents, scorpions, and other noxious reptiles, throwing them into it. On his head a crown of glory; on his right the sun, and on his left the moon, and in his hand a ring, with the twelve signs of the zodiac. Before the coffin, an olive tree sprouted forth, under the branches of which different kind of animals were collected. On the left, and a little further back, a high mountain was seen, with *seven* golden towers supporting the sky. A hand stretched forth from this sky, poured out light, and pointed with his fingers to the olive tree. There was also the figure of a man, whose head was in the sky, and whose feet were on the earth. His hands and feet were bound. Before the Lord stood seven censers, two pots, a vase filled with perfumes, spices, and a bottle with a long neck (retort), containing storax. The hieroglyphic representing day, was under his right foot, and the hieroglyphic representing night, under his left. Before the Lord was laid, on a high desk, the book of universal nature, whereon a representation and names of the planets, the constellations, the stations, and every thing that is found in the highest heaven, was painted. There was also an urn filled half with earth and half with sand, (viz. the hieroglyphics of earth and sand being represented therein). A suspended ever-burning lamp, dates, olives, and   in a vase of emerald. A table of black bazalt with *seven* lines, the four elements, the figure of a man carrying away a dead body, and a dog upon a lion.

These, O brother, are the mysterious keys to the treasures of secrets, of ancient and modern knowledge. The wise may guess the whole from a part. It is impossible to embrace here the whole extent of this knowledge. We have here stated the ground of the business, giving the representation of things in general, their ends, courses, movements, turns, and returns, so that thou mightest easily and by degrees distinguish the one from the other, and at last become master of all the secrets of the world. These hints are sufficient for him who has organs, and an understanding heart.

Here follows one of the hidden alphabets above mentioned (see orig. p. 129).

The next following alphabet was used by the Sabeans in their talismans, magical alarm-posts, and astrological conjuration tables.

Agathodaimon says, that it is from this source he drew the art of his talismans, in which he is unparalleled among either ancients or moderns. Learn, therefore, and comprehend this alphabet. (see orig. p. 130.)

The Chaldeans were the wisest men of their times, being well acquainted with every science and art. Their first equals and rivals were the *Curds*. But, however, there is as great a difference between these two nations, as between a *glow worm* and a *fixed star*.* The first superiority the *Curds* had over them, was in agriculture and botany. They pretended to descend from the sons of *Bineshad*, and to have got possession of the books of *Adam* on agriculture, and of the books of *Safrith* and *Coothami*. They pretended to have all the seven antediluvian books inspired by heaven.

They pretended to possess the art of magic and

---

* Being impossible to render in English the likeness of sounds between *turab* and *thura*, it has been thought proper to translate *glow-worm* and *fixed star*, instead of *dust* and *Pleiades*.

talismans, but this is not so; for all these sciences were handed down to them from the Chaldeans, who first cultivated them. This pretension to the antiquity of their learning, is the reason of the inveterate hatred between the Chaldeans and *Curds*.

The oldest Chaldean alphabet (see orig. p. 132).
Another Chaldean alphabet (see orig. p. 133).
Another old unknown alphabet (see orig. p. 134).

This the Curds falsely pretend to be the alphabet, in which *Bínúshád* and *Mássí Súráti* composed all their scientific and mechanical works.

We are ignorant to what alphabet these letters belong, as we never could make out the language which they express; but I saw at Bagdad, thirty-three inscriptions written in this alphabet.

During my stay at Damascus, I met with two books, one of them *on the culture of the vine and the palm tree*, the other *on water, and the means of finding it out in unknown ground*. I translated them both from the Curdic language into Arabic, for the benefit of mankind. This is the reason this treatise was not finished before. I finished it at last, with Heaven's assistance, after one and twenty years, and have, by the grace of God, attained the object proposed. I deposited it in the treasury of the *Calif Abd-ul-malik bin Marwán:* be his reign glorious, and may he be the everlasting column of the faith!

Tuesday, the third of the month of *Ramazán,* in the year two hundred and forty-one after the *Hijrah.*

Praised be God!

THE first copy of the manuscript before us, was taken from the original by *Hasan Bin Faraj, Bin Ali, Bin Dáwud, Bin Sinán, Bin Thábat, Bin Karra al Harráni, Al Bábali, An Núkáni,* Tuesday the seventh of the month of *Rabi-ul-ákhir,* in the year four hundred and thirteen of the *Hijrah;* and this copy (the one from which this was printed), which was made from it, was begun Monday the second of the month of *Muharram,* in the year of the *Hijrah,* one thousand, one hundred, and sixty-six. And it was finished on Friday, the tenth of the month of *Jamádi ul Akhir,* of the same year.

FINIS.

Printed by W. Bulmer and Co. Cleveland-row.

شوق المستهام في معرفة رموز الأقلام

الحمد لله وكفى
وسلام على عباده الذين اصطفى. امين.
وبعد فانه لما سُئلي من لاترد دعوته اذا جمع له
اصول الاقلام. التي تداولتها الامم الماضية من
الفضلا والحكما السالفين. والفلاسفة العارفين
ممارمزوا بها كتبهم وعلومهم. لينتفع به الطالبين و
الراغبين للعلوم الحكمية. والاسرار الربانية ذاكراً
القلم برسمه القديم. واسمه المشهور وشرح حروفه
بالقلم العربي تحته بالمداد الاحمر. ليمتاز عن الاخر.
❖ ورتبته على ابواب وسميته شوق المستهام ❖
❖ في معرفة رموز الاقلام. ❖
❖ وبالله المستعان ❖
❖ تم ❖

الباب الأول

في معرفة الاقلام الثلاثة
اي الكوفي . والمغربي . والهندي .

الفصل الاول من الباب الاول في معرفة القلم الكوفي

الكوفي الذي وضعه سيدنا اسمعيل عليه السلام. وهو اول من تكلم بالعربية وكتب وقد تنوع وصار تسعة انواع والاصل فيها المسمي بالسرياني وهذه

وهذه صورة القلم الكوفي المسمّى بالسوري كما تراه

ث . ح . ج . د . ه . و . ز . ع
ا . ب . ج . د . ه . و . ز . ع

ط . ي . ك . ل . م . ن
ط . ي . ك . ل . م . ن

س . ع . ف . ص . ق
س . ع . ف . ص . ق

ر . ش . ت . ث . خ . ذ
ر . ش . ت . ث . خ . ذ

ض . ظ . غ
ض . ظ . غ

الفصل

الفصل الثاني من الباب الأول في معرفة القلم المغربي وهو الأندلسي كما ترى صورته هكذا

ا . ب . ت . ث . ج . ح . خ .
ا . ب . ت . ث . ج . ح . خ .

د . ذ . ر . ز . ط . ظ . ك .
د . ذ . ر . ز . ط . ظ . ك .

ل . م . ن . ص . ض . ع .
ل . م . ن . ص . ض . ع .

غ . ف . ف . س . ش .
غ . ف . ق . س . ش .

ه . و . لا . ي .
ه . و . لا . ي .

الفصل

الفصل الثالث من الباب الاول في معرفة القلم الهندي وهو ثلثة انواع
النوع الاول منها

ايقع .   بكر .   جلش .
١ ١·· ١··   ٢ ٢· ٢··   ٣ ٣· ٣··

دمت .   هنث .   وسخ .
٤ ٤· ٤··   ٥ ٥· ٥··   ٦ ٦· ٦··

زعد .   حفض .   طصظ .
٧ ٧· ٧··   ٨ ٨· ٨··   ٩ ٩· ٩··

الفرع

النوع الثاني من الهندي

١٠ ٢٠ ٣٠ ٤٠ ٥٠ ٦٠ ٧٠ ٨٠ ٩٠
ا۰ ب۰ ج۰ د۰ ه۰ و۰ ز۰ ح۰ ط۰

أ۰ ٢۰ ٣۰ ٤۰ ٥۰ ٦۰ ٧۰ ٨۰ ٩۰
ي۰ ك۰ ل۰ م۰ ن۰ س۰ ع۰ ف۰ ص۰

أ۰ ٢۰ ٣۰ ٤۰ ٥۰ ٦۰ ٧۰ ٨۰ ٩۰
ق۰ ر۰ ش۰ ت۰ ث۰ خ۰ ذ۰ ض۰ ظ۰ غ۰

النوع

النوع الثالث من القلم الهندي

٩ . ٢ . ٨ . ٧ . ٦ . ٥ . ٤ . ٣ . ٢ . ٩
١ . ب . ج . د . ه . و . ز . ح . ط

ي . ك . ل . م . ن . س . ع . ف . ص

ق . ر . ش . ت . ث . خ . ذ . ض . ظ . غ

الباب

الباب الثاني

في الاقلام السبعة المشهورة
الفصل الاول من الباب الثاني في
القلم السرياني

ܠܐ . ܣ . ܐ . ܗ . ܚ . ܕ . ܕ . ܓ . ܒ . ܐ .
ط ح ز و ه د ج ب ا

ܩ . ܛ . ܗ . ܥ . ܢ . ܡ . ܠ . ܟ . ܝ .
ف ع س ن م ل ك ي

ܐ . ܨ . ܦ . ܨ . ܣ . ܬ .
ص ق ر ش ت

الفصل

الفصل الثاني من الباب الثاني في القلم النبطي القديم

| ا | ب | ج | د | ه | و | ز | ح | ط |

| ي | ك | ل | م | ن | س | ع | ف |

| ص | ق | ر | ش | ت | ث | خ | ذ |

| ض | ظ | غ |

الفصل

الفصل الثالث من الباب الثاني في القلم العبراني

א . ב . ג . ד . ה . ו . ז . ח . ט .
ا   ب ج د   ه   و   ز   ح   ط

י . ך . ל . מ . נ . ס . ע .
ي ك ل م ن   س   ع

פ . צ . ק . ר . ש . ת .
ف ص ق   ر   ش   ت

الفصل

الفصل الرابع من الباب الثاني في القلم البرباوي

ا	ب	ت	ث	ج	ح
ش	س	ز	ذ	د	خ
غ	ع	ظ	ط	ض	ص
م	ل	ق	ك	ف	
ي	لا	و	ۿ	ن	

الفصل

الفصل الخامس من الباب الثاني
في القلم لقمي

ⵋ · ⵎ · ◇ · ⵔ · ⵚ · ⵋ
ا   ب   ج   د   و   ز

·ⵋ · ▯ · ▯ · ╫ · ⵝ · ⵋ·
ح   م   ل   ك   ي   ط   م

· ⵋ · ⵔ · ⵋ · ⵔ · ⵋ · ⵋ
ن   س   ع   ف   ص   ق   ر

ⵋ: ⵋ · ⵔ · ⵋ · Ａ : ⵋ · ◇ · ⵔ · ⵋ·
ش   ت   ث   خ   ذ   ض   ظ   غ

الفصل

الفصل السادس من الباب الثاني في القلم المسند

ههـ . ᗈ . ᴫᴫ . 𐩴 . ᖇᖇ . 𐩱 .
١   ب   ت   ث   ج   ح

⟃ . 𐩱 . ⊕ . ⊙ . ∧ . < . ⊥ .
خ   د   ذ   ر   ز   س   ش

ട . 𐩯 . ⊕ . 𐩯 . ⟋ . 𐩡 . 𐩰 .
ص   ض   ع   غ   ف   ق   ط   ظ

⊐ . ⊓ . ⋏ . ⋞ . ᒣ . ᑎ . ᖶ .
ك   ل   م   ن   ء   و   ي

الفصل

الفصل السابع من الباب الثاني في القلم المنسي باليوناني قلم الحكما

A · B · Γ · h · O · Z · H · t ·
ا · ب · ج · د · و · ز · ح · ط ·

I · K · L · M · N · Ц · q ·
ي · ك · ل · م · ن · س · ع ·

H · R · Σ · m · Φ · Ξ · Ω ·
ث · ت · ش · ر · ق · ص · ف ·

ᗰ · ɗ ·
ذ · غ ·

الباب

الباب الثالث

في معرفة الاقلام الحكما السبعة المشهورين.
وهم
هرمس. واقليمون. وافلاطون. وفيتاغورس. و
اسقلينوس. وسقراط. وارسطوس.
الفصل الأول من الباب الثالث في قلم هرمس كما ترى

| ا | ب | ج | د | ه | و | ز |

| ح | ط | ى | ك | ل | م | ن |

| س | ع | ف | ص | ق | ر | ش | ت |

الفصل

الفصل الثاني من الباب الثالث
صفة قلم الحكيم اقليمون صاحب العجايب والعلم

ا ب ج د ه و ز ح

ط ي ك ل م ن س

ع ف ص ق رش ت

الفصل

الفصل الثالث من الباب الثالث
في صفة قلم الحكيم افلاطون

ا ب ج د ه و ز ح ط

ي ك ل م ن س ع ف ص

ق ر ش ت

الفصل

الفصل الرابع من الباب الثالث
في صفة قلم الحكيم فيثاغورس الوحيد

ﻫ	ד	ع	ص	ك	ں	П	Ш	H
ا	ب	ج	د	ه	و	ز	ح	

ى ك ل م ن س ع ف
ط

ص ق ر ش ت

الفصل

الفصل الخامس من الباب الثالث
في صفة قلم الحكيم اسقليبوس

سا	۶		ه	م	۶	۶
ا	ب	ج	د	ه	و	ز	ح

| ں | ⌇ | | ص | ⊂ | ع | ط |
| ن | م | ل | ك | ي | ط |

| ھ | ه | | لله | ≯ | ع | ھ |
| ق | س | ص | ف | ع | س |

| ـ | ▭ | ⊬ | وھ |
| ر | ش | ت |

الفصل

الفصل السادس من الباب الثالث
في صفة قلم الحكيم سقراط

ا ب ج د ه و

ز ح ط ي ك ل م

ن س ع ف ص

ذ خ ث ت ش ر ق

الفصل

الفصل السابع من الباب الثالث
في صفة قلم الحكيم ارسطوس

൧ . ⏃ . ⋝ . ᨻ . ⊙ . ⅄ . ⟡ . ⵁ . ⊐ . ⵤ .
ا   ب   ج   د   ه   و   ز   ح   ط

ഛ . ൦ഛ . ⰽ . Ⅲ . ⱷ . WW . ⋡ . ⚠ . ⚯ .
ي   ك   ل   م

ಎ . ⱷ . ᚛ . + . ⵕ . 🏛 . ⊢ . ⵕ .
ن   س   ع   ص   ق

ⰽⰽ . °ം . ⊞ . ᚁ . ⰻⰻⰻ . Ɛ .
ر   ش   ت   ث   خ   ذ

الباب

الباب الرابع

من شوق المستهام في معرفة رموز الاقلام
في ذكر الاقلام التي ظهرت بعد هذه السبعة. و
اسم واضعها من الحكما الذين تقدموا واشتهرو
ابالعلوم والمعارف. كل ياتي علي ترتيبه. فافهم.
الفصل الاول من الباب الرابع
في صفة قلم الحكيم بليناس

۳ . ⲕ . ⲅ . ⲅ . ⲕ . Ⳁ . ⵝ . ⵣ .
ا ب ت ت ث ج ج خ

د . لـ . ع . ۲۰ . ⲥ . ⲕ . ⲧ . ⲙ .
د ذ ر ز س ش ص ض ط

⳿ . ⳍ . ∩ . ⲗ . ⲑ . ٩ . ⵐ . ⲟ .
ظ ع غ ف ق ك ل م ن ه

ⵜ . ⲥ . ⳓ .
و ي لا

الفصل

الفصل الثاني من الباب الرابع
في صفة القلم البرباوي لسوريد الحكيم وهو عجيب

ﻙ	⌐	⋎	⌐	U	⊐	⋏
ا	ب	ت	ث	ج	ح	خ
د	ذ					

| ࠀ | ⋒ | ⋈ | ψ | ⋎ | ⋏ | ⌐ |
| ر | ز | س | ش | ص | ض | ط | ظ |

| ⋐ | H | ⋓ | ⋈ | A | ⋎ | ⊢ |
| ع | غ | ف | ق | ك | ل | م |

| ⋜ | ⋈ | = | ▽ | ᛏ | ⋒ |
| ن | ء | و | لا | ي |

الفصل

الفصل الثالث من الباب الرابع
في صفة القلم الذي وضعه
للحكيم فرنجيوش الفيلسوف
وقد لغز به كتب الحكمة

| ا | ب | ت | ث | ج | ح | خ |

| د | ذ | ر | ز | س | ش | ص | ض | ط | ظ |

| ع | غ | ف | ق | ك | ل | م |

| ن | ه | و | لا | ي |

الفصل

الفصل الرابع من الباب الرابع
في القلم المعلق الذي وضعه
للحكيم بطليموس اليوناني كماتري

۸. ۶. ۲. ٪. ۶. ڮ. ⊻. ۵. ة. ۶. ج.

ا   ب   ت   ث   ج   ح   خ   د   ذ   س

٤. ۲. ط. ه. ㎜. ۹. ک. ۶. م. سع. سع.

ه   ص   ض   ط   ظ   ع   غ   ف   ق

۴. ح. ۴. س. سع. سر. 3. ر. م. ل.

ق   ك   ل   م   ن   ه   و   لا   ي

الفصل

الفصل الخامس من الباب الرابع
في صفة القلم المربوط للحكيم
مرقونس وقد رمز به كتب الطلسمات

ظ . ٯ . ۷ . ص . د . ۴ . ۴ . ۴ . ۸ .
ا   ب   ت   ث   ج   ح   خ   د   ذ

ڡ . ₪ . X . ۸ . ۴ . ۴ . ۵ . ۷ . ⌐ .
س   ش   ص   ض   ط   ظ   ع   غ   ف

مح . سم . ۴ . ۴ . ۴ . ۹ . □ . ٯ . ع . مع .
ق   ك   ل   م   ن   ه   و   لا   ي

الفصل

الفصل السادس من الباب الرابع
في صفة القلم الجرجاني للحكيم مريانوس

ا   ب   ت   ث   ج   ح   خ

د   ذ   ر   ز   س   ش   ص

ض   ط   ظ   ع   غ   ف   ق

ك   ل   م   ن   ه   و   ي

الفصل

الفصل السابع من الباب الرابع
في صفة القلم النبطي القديم

I · ﻣ · لا · ؟ · ۱ · و · ﺳﺎ · ۸ · O · ⊕ · ᒪ · X ·
ا   ب   ت   ث   ج   ح   خ   د   ذ   ر   ز

ᒥ · O · ᦉ · ᒷ · Gا · H+ · ᦉ ·
س   ﻫ   ص   ض   ط   ظ   ع

· ᵯ · لما · ڪ · ۴ · ᵧ · ᘕ · □ · ϒ · ܒ · ﻋﺪ ·
غ   ف   ق   ك   ل   م   ن   ه   و

· ᒡ · ᦉ ·
لا   ي

الفصل

الفصل الثامن من الباب الرابع
في صفة القلم الأحمر الذي وضعه للحكيم مغنيس الفيلسوف

| ا | ب | ت | ث | ج | ح | خ | د | ذ |

| ر | ز | س | ش | ص | ض | ط | ظ | ع |

| غ | ف | ق | ك | ل | م | ن | ه | و | لا | ي |

الفصل

الفصل التاسع من الباب الرابع
في صفة القلم الطلسمي للحكيم غاميغا شير
الفيلسوف اليوناني

ᒣ · H · X · Ɩ · Ζ · V · · · ɧ · ɓ · ᒣ ·
ا ب ت ث ج ح خ د ذ ر

۳ · ᒼ · ⌂ · ⌐ · ⊔ · □ · ∫ · ⊑ · ⌐ · 9 ·
ز س ش ص ض ط ظ ع غ

ه · ∧ · ↄ · ⊇ · ᒼ · ى · ه · ·
ف ق ك ل م ن ة و

· · · ·
لا ي

الفصل

الفصل العاشر من الباب الرابع
في صفة القلم الرمزي الذي وضعه
الحكيم هلياوش اليوناني واصطلح
عليه في كتبه

ا ب ج د ه و ز ح ط ي

ك ل م ن س ع ف ص ق

ش ت ث خ ذ ض غ

الفصل

الفصل الحادي عشر من الباب الرابع في صفة قلم للحكيم قسطوجيس اليوناني وقد كتب بهذا القلم ثلثماية وستين كتاباً في علم الصنعة الالهية . وفي علم الطلسم . و النيرنج و السحر . و دعوات الكواكب . و النجوم . وتسخير الروحانية .

ﻫ . ﻁ . ت . ت . ۷ . ﻍ . ق . ۴ . ﻝ .
ا ب ج د ﻫ و ز ح ط

ق . ص . ﻫ . ۹ . ع . م . ل . ت . x .
ي ك ل م ن س ع ف ص ق

غ . ظ . ض . ذ . خ . ث . ت . ش . ر
ر ش ت ث خ ذ ض ظ غ

الفصل

الفصل الثاني عشر من الباب الرابع في صفة قلم للحكيم هرمس ابو طاط الذي كتب الصنعة الشريفة . وصنع باقليم الصعيد كنوزاً وبراري ونواويس كاهنية له و لولده . ورصدها ورمزها بهذا القلم . الذي استخرجه من السرب المظلم

ا ب ج د ه و ز ح ط ي

ك ل م ن س ع ف ص ق

ر ش ت ث خ ذ ض ظ غ

الفصل

الفصل الثالث عشر من الباب الرابع

في صفة قلم للحكيم قلفطريوس صاحب السميا و القلفطربات و الطلسم و النيرنجات و السحر و الدك و السعيدة. و قد تداولت الحكما و الفلاسفة هذا القلم في كتبها و علومها دون غيرها من الاقلام بكثرة خواصها

ا ب ج د هـ و ز ح ط

ي ك ل م ن س ع ف

ص ق ر ش ت ث خ ذ

ض ظ غ ع

الفصل

الفصل الرابع عشر من الباب الرابع
في صفة قلم الحكيم سيوريانوس
الذي الف كتب الفلك . واسرار النجوم .
والطلسمات وخواصها . والرصد . وعمل
خواتيم الكواكب . وتسخير مروحانياتها وجلبها

ا . ب . ج . د . ه . و . ز . ح . ط

ي . ك . ل . م . ن . س . ع . ف

ص . ق . ر . ش . ت . ث . خ

ذ . ض . ظ . غ

الفصل

الفصل الخامس عشر من الباب الرابع
في صفة قلم الحكيم فيلاوس
الذى وضع الدخنات العجيبة . و التراكيب الغريبة . و الطلسم . و النيرنج . و السحر . وصنع كنزًا بالاهرام . و رصده بالارصاد العجيبة

| ا | ب | ج | د | ه | و | ز | ح | ط |

| ي | ك | ل | م | ن | س | ع | ف | ص |

| ق | ر | ش | ت | ث | خ | ذ |

| ض | ظ | غ |

الفصل

الفصل السادس عشر من الباب الرابع
في صفة قلم الحكيم ديسقوريدوس
وهو المشجر الذي كتب كتاب الاعشاب
والنبات . وخواصها ومنافعها ومضارها و
اسرارها . وقد تداوله الحكما من بعده
في الكتب .

𐩰 𐩰 𐩰 𐩰 𐩰 𐩰 𐩰 𐩰 𐩰 𐩰
ا ب ج د ه و ز ح ط ي ك

𐩰 𐩰 𐩰 𐩰 𐩰 𐩰 𐩰 𐩰 𐩰
ل م ن س ع ف ص ق ر ش

𐩰 𐩰 𐩰 𐩰 𐩰 𐩰 𐩰
ت ث خ ذ ض ظ غ

الفصل

الفصل السابع عشر من الباب الرابع
في صفة القلم الداودي

وهذا القلم كثير الاستعمال ببلاد الهند.
يستعملونها للحكما في كتب الطب والحكمة
وكتب السياسة وهو مشهور

X · V · ¥ · W · ٪ · H · < · ح · ٩ · T ·
ا   ب ت ث ج ح خ د ذ ر

ج · ∽ · ⊥ · V · ¥ · ⊿ · △ · ⊿ · ⊥ · ∥ · ≈ ·
ز س ش ص ض ط ظ ع غ ف

⊲ · ≅ · ل · ∘∘ · ≥ · ه · ٪ · H ·
ق ك ل م ن ه و لا ي

الفصل

الفصل الثامن عشر من الباب الرابع
في صفة قلم للحكيم ذيهقراطيس
وهذا القلم كان مقبولاً عند حكما اليونان.
يلغزون ويرمزون به كتبهم. ويزعمون
ان هذا القلم اهدته له
روحانية كوكب عطارد. وهو في السرب المظلم.

Ɔ . ϑ . G . ꝏ . ل . H . ㅜ . ᐁ . Ͻ . ᒋ .
ا ب ت ث ج ح خ د ذ ر

ʎ . ⊏ . ⊨ . ᒪᒥ . ⊟ . Ⅰ . ⅃ . ⁊ . ᓀ .
ز س ش ص ض ط ظ ع غ

ᒷ . 8 . ᐩ . ϙ . ᑌ . □ . ᐢ . ᐢ . ᕮ .
ف ق ك ل م ن ه و ي

الفصل

الفصل التاسع عشر من الباب الرابع
في صفة قلم حكما الاقباط

وأكثر ما يرمزون به كتب الدفاين والمطالب والكنوز والخبايا . وكتب الصنعة الشريفة الالهية . وهذا القلم مخترعه قفطريم من اولاد نوح عليه السلام . وقد يستعمل في الحساب .

ا ب ج د ه و ز ح ط ي ك ل

م ن س ع ف ص ق ر ش ت

ث خ ذ ض ظ غ

الفصل

الفصل العشرون من الباب الرابع
في صفة القلم الفرغاني

وهذا القلم اخترعه سبعة من حكما الروم. وكتبوا به كتباً كثيرة في علم السميا والكيميا والطب. وكان رئيسهم ديوجانس الاكبر ملك الروم. واشتهر في زمانه ونسي.

ا	ب	ج	د	ه	و	ز	ح	ط

ي	ك	ل	م	ن	س	ع

ف	ص	ق	ر	ش	ت	ث	خ	ذ

ض	ظ	غ

الفصل

الفصل الحادي والعشرون من الباب الرابع في صفة قلم الحكيم زوسيم العبري وهو القلم الزي اصطلح عليه حكما العبرايين من القدماء . ورمزوا به كتب الحكمة الشريفة. وكانت موجودة في القدس .

الفصل

الفصل الثاني و العشرون من الباب الرابع
في صفة قلم الحكيم مارشول
صاحب العجايب و الغرايب الذي ألف
الكتب في العلوم و الفنون.

ﺍ . ب . ج . د . ه . و . ز . ح . ط . ي

ك . ل . م . ن . س . ع . ف . ص . ق . ر

ش . ت . ث . خ . ذ . ض . ظ . غ

الفصل

الفصل الثالث و العشرون من الباب الرابع في صفة قلم للحكيم ارغانيس اليوناني صاحب التراكيب العجيبة . والاخلاط و الدخن الغريبة . وامثال الترياقات الملوكية . والادوية العجيبة الفعل والتاثيرات

ا ب ت ث ج ح خ د ذ ر

ز س ش ص ض ط ظ ع غ

ف ق ك ل م ن و ي

الفصل

الفصل الرابع والعشرون من الباب الرابع في صفة القلم المتجر الطبيعي لافلاطون الحكيم ذكرانة جرب لكل حرف خواص ومنافع لا مورشتي م

۲ . ۷ . ۲ . ۴ . ۴ . ۴ . ۴ . ۴ . ۴
۱   ب ج د ه و ز ح ط ي

۴ . ۴ . ۴ . ۲ . ۷ . ۷ . ۴ . ۴ . ۴
ك ل م ن س ع ف ص ق

۴ . ۴ . ۴ . ۴ . ۴ . ۴ . ۴ . ۴ . ۴ . ۴
ر ش ت ث خ ذ ض ظ غ ع ه

الباب

الباب الخامس

من كتاب شوق المستهام في معرفة رموز الاقلام في معرفة اقلام الكواكب السبعة من زحل الي القمر.

الفصل الاول من الباب الخامس في صفة معرفة قلم كوكب زحل

ا ب ج د ه و ز ح ط

ي ك ل م ن س ع ف ص

ق ر ش ت ث خ ذ ض ظ غ

الفصل

الفصل الثاني من الباب الخامس
في صفة قلم كوكب المشتري
وهيئته كما تري فافهم

ا ب ج د ه و ز ح

ط ي ك ل م ن س ع

ف ص ق ر ش ت ث خ

ذ ض ظ غ

الفصل

الفصل الثالث من الباب الخامس
في صفة قلم الحكيم بهرام وهو قلم
كوكب المريخ كما تراه

ا ب ج د ه‍ و ز ح ط

ي ك ل م ن س ع ف ص

ق ر ش ت ث خ ذ ض

ظ غ

الفصل

الفصل الرابع من الباب الخامس
في صفة قلم كوكب الشمس سلطان الفلك

ا ب ج د هـ و ز ح ط

ي ك ل م ن س ع ف ص ق

ر ش ت ث خ ذ ض ظ غ

الفصل

الفصل الخامس من الباب الخامس
في صفة قلم كوكب الزهرة
اناهيد مطريه الفلك كماتري

ا ب ج د ه و ز ح طي ك

ل م ن س ع ف ص ق ر

ش ت ث خ ذ ض ظ ع

الفصل

الفصل السادس من الباب الخامس
في صفة قلم كوكب عطارد وهو هرمس
كاتب الفلك كماتري

ا ب ج د هـ و ز ح ط

ي ك ل م ن س ع ف

ص ق ر ش ت ث خ ذ

ض ظ غ

الفصل

الفصل السابع من الباب الخامس
في صفة قلم كوكب القمر كماتري

ا . ب . ج . د . ه . و . ز . ح . ط

ي . ك . ل . م . ن . س . ع . ف

ص . ق . ر . ش . ت . ث . خ . ذ

ض . ظ . غ

الباب

الباب السادس

من شوق المستهام في معرفة ورموز الاقلام في ذكر اقلام البروج الاثنى عشر. من الحمل الي الحوت.

الفصل الاول من الباب السادس في صفة قلم برج الحمل الناري الربيعي المنسوب للمريخ

ا . ب . ج . د . ه . و . ز . ح . ط
ي . ك . ل . م . ن . س . ع . ف . ص
ق . ر . ش . ت . ث . خ . ذ . ض . ظ . غ

الفصل

الفصل الثاني من الباب السادس
في صفة قلم برج الثور وكوكبه الزهرة

| ﻁ | ح | ز | و | ه | د | ج | ب | ا |

| ض | ف | ع | س | ن | م | ل | ك | ي |

| ق | ر | ش | ت | ث | خ | ذ | ض |

| غ | ظ |

الفصل

الفصل الثالث من الباب السادس
في صفة قلم برج الجوزا وكوكبه عطارد

ط	ح	ز	و	ه	د	ج	ب	ا

ق	ص	ف	ع	س	ن	م	ل	ك	ي

غ	ظ	ض	ذ	خ	ث	ت	ش	ر

الفصل

الفصل الرابع من الباب السادس
في صفة قلم برج السرطان وكوكبه القمر

| ا | ب | ج | د | ه | و | ز | ح | ط | ي | ك |

| ل | م | ن | س | ع | ف | ص | ق | ر | ش |

| ت | ث | خ | ذ | ض | ظ | غ |

الفصل

الفصل لخامس من الباب السادس
في صفة قلم برج الاسد وكوكبه الشمس

ا ب ج د ه و ز ح ط

ي ك ل م ن س ع ف ص ق

ر ش ت ث خ ذ ض ظ غ

الفصل

الفصل السادس من الباب السادس
في صفة قلم برج السنبلة وعطارد

ا ب ج د ه و ز ح

ط ي ك ل م ن س ع

ف ص ق ر ش ت ث خ ذ

ض ظ غ

الفصل

الفصل السابع من الباب السادس
في صفة قلم برج الميزان

ا ب ج د هـ و ز

ح ط ي ك ل م ن س ع

ف ص ق ر ش ت ث خ

ذ ض ظ غ

الفصل

الفصل الثامن من الباب السادس
في صفة قلم برج العقرب

و هذا القلم من جملة الاقلام المكتومة في دخاير الكلدانيين . و قد رمزوا به كتب الارصاد و الاسرار التي تتعلق بكوكب المريخ . الذي فاضت روحانية ما رشميناعلي الكاهن العارف اربياسيوس النبطي.

ا	ب	ج	د	ه	و	ز	ح	ط
ي	ك	ل	م	ن	س	ع	ف	ص
ق	ر	ش	ت	ث	خ	ذ	ض	ظ	غ

تم قلم برج العقرب

الفصل

الفصل التاسع من الباب السادس
في صفة قلم برج القوس وكوكبه المشتري

ا ب ج د هـ و ز ح ط ي

ك ل م ن س ع ف ص ق

ر ش ت ث خ ذ ض ظ غ

تم قلم برج القوس

الفصل

الفصل العاشر من الباب السادس
في صفة قلم برج الجدي وزحل

و هذا القلم مما اختص به حكما بابل و الفرس و اخفوه . ثم ظهر بعد انقراضهم في كتب اسرارهم و خبايا كنوزهم التي نهبتها اليونان . ثم استعمله حكما مصر في علم الفلك

ا . ب . ج . د . ه . و . ز . ح

ط . ي . ك . ل . م . ن . س . ع

ف . ص . ق . ر . ش . ت . ث . خ . ذ

ض . ظ . غ

الفصل

الفصل الحادي عشر من الباب السادس
في صفة قلم برج الدلو وكوكبه زحل
وهو من جملة الاقلام المنسوبة للكلدانيين
والصابيين وبه رتبوا كتب صلواتهم ودعواتهم
واسرار نواميسهم الخاصة . مما فاضت به
عليهم روحانيته .

ا ب ج د ه و ز ح ط

ي ك ل م ن س ع ف ص

ق ر ش ت ث خ ذ ض ظ

غ ني ويم

الفصل

الفصل الثاني عشر من الباب السادس
في صفة قلم برج الحوت

ا ب ج د و ز ح ط ي

ك ل م ن س ع ف ص ق

ر ش ت ث خ ذ ض ظ غ

تم الباب

تم الباب السادس في ذكر اقلام البروج الاثني عشر باصولها. كماقد اصطلح عليه القدماء مما وجدناهم في كتبهم و دخايرهم. و وضعناها في هذا الكتاب. ليقتبس منه كل طالبٍ لبيب ما يخصه من الاسرار و النكت.

الباب

الباب السابع

من شوق المستهام في معرفة رموز الاقلام في ذكر اقلام الملوك التي تقدمت من ملوك السريان . والهرامسة . والفراعنة . والكنعانيين . والكلدانيين . والنبط . والاكراد . والكسدانيين . والفرس . والقبط .

الفصل

الفصل الأول من الباب السابع
في صفة قلم الملك برِدويس السرياني

وقد رمز جميع كتبه و اسراره بهذا القلم الذي اخترعه من دقايق للحكمة الالهية و النواميس الطبيعية . و هذه صفته كما ترى .

ص . ڡ . ▢ . ⋈ . ▭ . ⋄ . ⊠
ا ب ت ث ج ح خ د ذ

▦ . ⋉ . ⊡ . ط . ظ . ض . ص . ش . س . ز . ر
ع ظ ط ض ص ش س ز ر

غ ف ق ك ل م ن ه

و لا ي

الفصل

الفصل الثاني من الباب السابع في ذكر قلم الملك وسيوث الفرعوني المصري الذي وضع الارصاد و الطلاسم العجيبة . وكلها بهذا القلم القديم الوضع .

ا ب ت ث ج ح خ د ذ ر ز

س ش ص ض ط ظ ع غ ف

ق ك ل م ن لا و ي

الفصل

الفصل الثالث من الباب السابع
في ذكر قلم الملك كيماس الهرمسي
الذي كتب في علم الفلك نحو مايتين كتاب
وفي الاسرار الطبيعية . وفي خواص النبات
و العقاقير . وصفته هكذا .

ا ب ت ث ج ح خ د ذ ر
ز س ش ص ض ط ظ ع غ ف
ق ك ل م ن ه و لا ي

الفصل

الفصل الرابع من الباب السابع
في ذكر قلم الملك مهراريش
وكان كاهناً بارعاً في العلوم الحكمية . والنو
اميس الالهية . والف كتباً كثيرة في ساير
الفنون . وهذا القلم من جملة اقلامه كما تري

ا ب ت ث ج خ د ذ ر

ز س ش ص ض ط ظ ع

غ ف ق ك ل م ن ه و ي

الفصل

الفصل الخامس من الباب السابع في ذكر قلم الملك طبرينوس الكاهن وهو من جملة الأقلام التي كانوا الفراعنة يكتبوا بها علي النواويس .

ا . ب . ت . ث . ج . ح . خ . د . ذ

ر . ز . س . ش . ص . ض . ط . ظ . ع . غ

ف . ق . ك . ل . م . ن . ه . و . ي

الفصل

الفصل السادس من الباب السابع في ذكر قلم الملك ديوس موس المصري أحد الفراعنة المشهورين بالكهانة السحر و انواع الطلسمات و النارنجات . و هذه صورته هكذا .

| أ | ب | ت | ج | ح | خ | د | ذ | ر | ز |

| س | ش | ص | ض | ط | ظ | ع | غ | ف |

| ق | ك | ل | م | ن | ه | و | ي |

الفصل

الفصل السابع من الباب السابع
في ذكر قلم الملك برهميوس المصري
هذا القلم من قديم الزمان كانت سحرا
فرعون و مصر تستعمله . ثم انتقل الي
كهنا بلاد الهند و الصين .

ا ب ت ث ج ح خ د ذ

ر ز س ش ص ض ط ظ ع

غ ف ق ك ل م ن ه

و ي

الفصل

الفصل الثامن من الباب السابع في ذكر قلم الملك صاᙏᙏ الكاهن وهو من السحرا السبعة . الذين كانوا ملوكاً وحكما وكهنا وسحرا وفلاسفة عبصر . وملكوها وعمروها . وبنوا فيها مدناً عظيمة الي الان .

ا . ب . ت . ث . ج . ح . خ . د . ذ . ر

ز . س . ش . ص . ض . ط . ظ . ع

غ . ف . ق . ك . ل . م . ن . ه . و

لا . ي

الفصل

الفصل التاسع من الباب السابع
في ذكر قلم الملك بلبيس
الذي بني مدينة طولها اربعة فراسخ .
و صنع فيها عجايب كثيره . و كتب بهذا
القلم كتباً كثيره . و هو هذا

ا ب ت ج ح خ د ذ ر ز

س ش ص ض ط ظ ع غ ف

ق ك ل م ن ه و ي

الفصل

الفصل العاشر من الباب السابع
في ذكر قلم الملك قفطريم المصري
صاحب الطلسمات و ارصاد العجيبة . و
الصور و الكنوز الغريبة . و كان هذا القلم
كتب به جميع العلوم و هذه صورته

ا ب ت ث ج خ د ذ ر

ز س ش ص ض ط ظ ع غ

ف ق ك ل م ه ن و ي

الباب

الباب الثامن

من كتاب شوق المستهام في معرفة رموز الاقلام

في ذكر اقلام الهرامسة مما اطلعنا عليه في كتب القدما. لان الهرامسة كل منهم وضع قلماً بحكمته و قوة فهمه. ليكتم به علومه واسراره. ليلا يطلع عليها غرابنا الحكمة. فلذلك قل في زماننا من يعرفها. لانهم وضعوها علي هية الرسم والمثال. بانواع الالات. والاشجار والنبات. والحيوانات. و الطيور. و بعض اجزا منها.

وبعض

و بعض صور من الكواكب والنجوم . فلذلك لاتعد كثرة و لاتحصى . مثل اقلام بلاد الهند و الصين فان لهم اقلاماً ليست كترتيبنا علي حروف الف بالحر . بل لهم في ذلك اصطلاحات لاتشبه راي اصحاب الخطوط و الاقلام . و انما خالفونا في الرسم و الترتيب لعلة ما وهي انهم عرفوا الاشيا الطبيعية بحسب عقولهم كما ينبغي . و راوا ان يرتبوا لكل مادة منها شكلاً مناسباً لماهيته . تدل بصورتها علي تلك الذات . و اما المذهب الثاني . اعتمد وا في رسمها علي القواعد الهندسية . و استنباطها من بعضها البعض . كالكوفي من السرياني . و العبراني من الكلداني .

واللاطيني

و اللاطيني من اليوناني . و غيرها من الاقلام الاصلية . و الاقلام الفرعية فانها في الغالب علي هذا النمط . فمن اراد ان يطلع علي حقايق فن الاقلام فليراجع كتاب حل الرموز و مفاتيح الكنوز . لجابر بن حيان الصوفي . فانه استوفي مايلزم هذه الصناعة من اللوازم تفصيلاً و اجمالاً . و انما مقصودنا في هذا الكتاب ذكرما اشتهر من اقلام الهرامسة مما رايناه . و اما رموزهم للخاصة فلم يعرفها احد في زماننا هذا .
و الله الموفق للصواب .

الفصل

الفصل الاول من الباب الثامن
في ذكر قلم للحكيم هرمس الاكبر
وهو القلم المكتوب علي البرابي . والهرمات .
والنواويس . والاحجار و الهياكل القديمة .
من زمن الفراعنة الاول . واعلم ان هذا القلم
ليس كساير الاقلام مرتباً علي الحروف . بل
هو رموز و اشارات مستخرجه بحسب ما
اصطلح عليه هرمس الاكبر . وهي رسوم و
اشكال لاتعد ولاتحصر . وانما وضعوها قاعدة
يستدل بها علي ذلك الشي المط . مثاله
يجعلون صورة شكل يدل على انه اسم الله
تعالي مطلقاً . فاذا اضافه شي من اسماء
الصفات . لحقوا بذلك الشي الاصلي جزاً من
شكل اخر . ويتموه بحسب ما ارادوا علي هذا
الوصف . وعلي هذه القاعدة الاتي بيان مثاله
كما

كما ستراه . وقد جعلنا على ثلثة مراتب دون العلويات . فاولاً نبدا بالاثار العلوية . و صور اشكالها الدالة على اسماذ واتها بلسانهم الهرمسي كما وجدناه . و هذه صورتها كما ترى .

الحي . العالم بكل خفي وظاهر المدبر لكل شي من المصنوعات العلوية و السفلية بارادته

مَلَك

كوكب • نجم • سما • شيطان • مَلَك

سحاب • نور • الظلمة • الدنيا

مريخ • مشتري • زحل • قمر • الهوا

عطارد • زهره • شمس • شمس

حمل • ثور • جوزا • سرطان

اسد

عقرب	ميزان	سنبله	اسد

نار	جدي	حوت	دلو	قوس

عناصر	تراب	ماء

فهذا ما وجدناه من الأشكال الهرمسية الدالة علي الآثار العلويّة. و حان لنا ان نذكر الثلثة مراتب التي و عدنا بذكرهم. اي نذكر كل مرتبة منها. وما وجدناه من الأسما و الأشكال في الهرمسية.

المرتبة

المرتبة الاولي

في ذكر الاسما الحيوانية و اشكالها مفرداً مفرداً. من ساير الانواع و افعالها و حركاتها.

| المراة | الرجل | الفقر | الغني | الموت | الحياه |

| الخطية | الشر | الخير | الردي | الطيب |

| الروح | العقل | البكا | الغم | الفرح |

| اليقظة | النوم | السكون | الحركة | الجسد |

البلادة

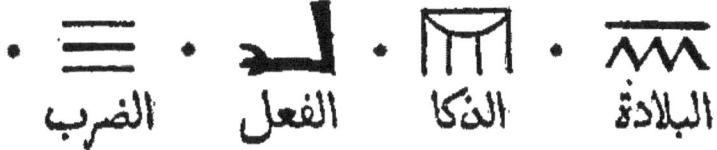

البلادة . الذكا . الفعل . الضرب

النسيان . الفهم . الخنوع . الارادة . الاطاعة

المكر . القتل . السجن . السّر

الخفي . المجنون . المريض . الطيّب . القوي

المودي . القطع . الصلب . الزمان

الساعة

الساعة · 〜 · ▬ · ⊕ · 👤 · 🐦 الغلط   الجهل العلم الدهر الساعة

· ☰ · ◣ · ▮ · ⊞ · ✕ · ◉
الحق الباطل العدد الهندسة الرياسة

· 〜 · ◇ · ▭ · V · ☽
الهدم البنا الحجر الشجر الجوهر

· ⊓ · ▮ · ⚱ · ⋈ · ⌐
العظم القرن الدم البلغم السودا

· 🐦 · D · ◊ · ⇨ · ⊤
الصفرا البياض الحمرة السواد الصفرة

الخضرة

العداوة الظلم الضيق الوسع الحضرة

الدخول الناموس والحكم الحرق العدل السرقة

الركوب الذهاب الدوا القيام الخروج

الكاهن الامام الخشوع الصلاة العبادة التدبير

الصيدلاني العارف الفاسد الصالح السلطنة

الفلسفة

الكذب · المخالفة · الفصاحة · الفلسفة

الوزن · الصنعة · الاسرار · الاسرار لخواص ·
الروحية   الطبيعية

والسيميا · السحر المخرقة · الطلسمات · علم الفلك
الاعلى

وهذا

و هذا الشكل بجملته عندهم هو السر المسمّى بهوميد وخروف بعني شرّ لاهوت طبيعة كلية العوالم . و يسمّى سرّ السرّ و المبدي و المعيد . و لهم في هذا الشكل كلام طويل لا يحويه هذا الكتاب . فمن اراد الاطلاع علي اسرار الهرامسة . فليراجع الكتاب

الكتاب الذي ترجمته من لساننا النبطي المسمى بكتاب شمس الشموس و قمر الاقمار. في كشف رموز الهرامسة و مالهم من الخفايا و الاسرار. فانه جمع فيه مالابد منه لمن اراد الوقوف علي اسرار هولاء القوم. وهذا اخرها وقفت عليه من صور الاشكال الحيوانية و بهختمنا المرتبة الاولي.

المرتبة الثانية

في ذكر صور الاشكال الدالة علي ذوات المفردات النباتية و انواعها. اعلم ايها الحكيم العارف. ان الهرامسة الخاصة لم يطلعوا علي اسرارهم غيرابناء جنسهم. خوفاً علي اسرارهم ليلا تضيع مع غيراهله من اولاد السفلة. و فساد العالم و خرابه. فجعلوا هذه الرموز ستراً

ستراً علي علومهم وكنوزهم ودخايرهم . وما وضعوه من الاشيا المكتومة التي لم يطلع عليها الّا اهلها من ابناء الحكمة . وكانوا مع هذا مذاهب اربعة . فالاول منهم يقال لهم الهرامسة الهومية وهم اولاد هرمس الاكبر الذين لم يتزوجوا بنسا من غير ابنا جنسهم . و لم يختلطوا بغريب ولم يختلط معهم غريب فلم احد ممن في العالم عرف رموزهم . ولم يطلع عليهم سواهم . وهم اصحاب الصحف الادريسية . والهياكل الروحانية . و برابي الحكمة . وقد قلّ نسلهم في زماننا هذا . وانتهوا في بعض الجزاير التي في حدود الصين . وهم علي ما كانوا عليه . الثاني الهرامسة البينا ولوزية و هم اولاد اخي هرمس اعني اسقليبيانوس . تزوجوا

تزوجوا وتناسلوا من اصلهم . ولم يشاركوا اهل زمانهم في شي ما . بل الناس كانت تحتاج لهم في الامور كلها . وكان الفرق بين الهومية وبين هولاء.. بالقرابين والدختات في روس الاهلة والبروج والفصول والمنازل . ولهم في كل فصل عيد سبعة ايام . واما الهومية ليس لهم في كلها شي سوي التوسلات بقرأت الصحف والعبادة والصوم . ولهم عيد في كل عام ثمانية وعشرين يوماً من ابتدا حلول الشمس برج الحمل . الي ثمام الثمانية و عشرين يوماً . فيقربون فيه القرابين و الدخنات وغير ذلك . ويقرون بوحدانية الباري تعالي . وانه الموجد لكل شي في الكاينات تبارك اسمه . واما هذه الطايفة ايضاً فانها لم تطلع

لم تطلع احدًا من الامم شيًا من الاسرار الخفية والدخائر الهرمسية . بل كانوا يتدا و لونه بينهم جيلًا جيلًا الي يومنا هذا . وكانوا اذا ولد لهم مولود فتاخذه امه و تذهب به الي كاهن من خدام الهيكل الذي اعدلا مَتحان المواليد . فتضع المولود علي عتبة الهيكل ولم تتكلم امه بكلام . فياتي الكاهن في يده طاسة من الذهب ملان ماء . و هو يقري عليه . و معه ستة اخرى . ويرشه بذلك الماء . فان تحرّك المولود و قلب وجهه لوجه العتبة . اخذه الكاهن بيده و ادخله الي بيت سِرّ داخل الهيكل . و يضعه علي تابوت مهيًا لذلك . و يبدوا يقراون ويجزون ساعة . ثم ياخذ الكاهن الريُّس منديلًا من ابريسم اخضر للانثي . و احمر للذكر

احمر للذكر. فيضعه علي وجه المولود. و يدخله في التابوت ويغلقه عليه. ثم يأخذ بيده عصا مثلث الراس من فضة مجوهر بالاحجار النفيسة. ويأتي امه وابيه واقاربه يقفون بالخضوع والذكر وثلاث التسابيح صامتين. ثم يضرب الكاهن التابوت بذلك العصا ثلاث مرات. و ينادي باسم الربّ الهك الذي كونك و انشاك بحكمة. انطق بسر طباعك الروحانية عن جميع حوادث حياتك. امين امين الي ابد الابدين ودهر الداهرين. ثم ايسجدوا الجميع سبع سجدات. و يرفعوا روسهم. فينطق المولود بالسلام و البركة. فيرد الريس عليه بالجواب. ثم يسأله ما اسمك. و ما قربانك. واي شي تريد لقيام اودك وتدبير معيشتك

معيشتك . و اي ساعة حليت بهذه البنية الشريفة . و الصورة الكريمة . وهل انت مقيم كاقرانك ام ضيف راحل . اسئلك بحق الله الحي القيوم الابدي الازلي . الذي له ما يزي و ما لايري . رب الارضين و السموات العلي . ان تجيبنا ونعاهدك علي ميثاقنا و ايماننا . انك بقيت في عالم الكون و الفساد . ان لا تظهر اسرارنا لغير جنسنا . فيجيبه المولود باسمه الحقيقي الذي سطرله في لوح الازل من المبدا الاول . و هو من ارباب الحكمة و العلوم . او من اختار الصنايع والحرف والفنون . او كاحد منهم . فينطق لهم بجميع ما ارادوا و طلبوا . وهم يسمعونه في الجواب . ويثبته عندد الكاهن ومنقوشا في لوح من حجر الكدان . ويعلقه في الهيكل

الهيكل . ثم يدعوله . يفتح باب التابوت وينحروا له بدخنته . ويذبحواله قربانه ان كان طيرًا او حيوانًا . ويحرقوا دمه ويطهّروا الجسد . ثم يلفوه في ازار ابيض لطيف . ماية وعشرين راقًا للذكر . وستين راقًا للاثني . ويجعلونه في انافخار . ويضعوه في بيرالقربان . ولهم في هذا امور تدل علي اسرار خفية لم يدركها احد سواهم . وهذا التابوت كالصندوق الصغير علي قدرالمولود . من خشب الزيتون مرصع بالذهب و الجواهر . واذا لم يظهر من المولود هذا السر العظيم . لم يدخلوه ولا يقبلوه . ويقولوا هذا لا يوتمن علي اسرارنا و خفايا امورنا . وربما يخرجونه من بين اظهرهم . ويقولوا ان هذا المولود مشترك فيه او مولود سو . فاذا اكبر المولود واراد

واراد الخروج من ملتهم فانه يموت الي ثلثة ايام ولهم ايضا سرّ اخر من اعظم اسرارهم . فاذا كان يوم عيدهم ياخذون سبع ثيران . وسبع حملان . ويطعمونهم النبات المعروف بحشيشة الزهره و تلج الملوك . و يسمونه بلسانهم شيكرك . فيعلفونهم بها سبعة ايام . ويسقونهم من الماء الطهور. هذه فاذا كان يوم الاسبوع كللون يتجانهم بالذهب وانواع الجواهر . ويجعلونهم مربوطين بسلاسل الذهب . ويبدون الكهنا يصلون ويسبحون ويقراون في الهيكل الكبير الجامع . و الناس في مراتبهم ساجدين لله خاشعين ثم يتقدم ريّس المذبح للقرابين . ويشير بالعصا المثلث للثيران وللحملان . فتتحلل قيودهم من غير فعل فاعل . ويتقدمون للذبح . ويمدون اعناقهم بارادتهم . فيذبحهم الريس . وياخذ الروس

الرؤس يجعلها علي تابوت الستر. يقربوا الاجساد محرقة بانواع الطيب. كالعود والعنبر والمصك والكافور واللوبان والاصطراك. يقوموا للصلاة الكبري. وقد ليس كل ذي زي زين. ودم يقراون الصحف. ثم يخروا ساجدين ساعة. ويرفعوا روسهم. فحنين يبتدي اول راس من المذبوحة يتكلم بجميع الحوادث التي تتبع في ذلك. ثم الثاني. ثم الثالث. هكذا حتي يتموا. فيثبت الكاهن جميع ما يسمعه. ويستعدوا لوقوعها. وهكذالهم امور لايعرف حقيقتها غيرهم. وكل هذه الاشيا تدل علي شدة كتمانهم لخفايا اسرارهم. ويقولون هكذا. امرنا ابونا ادم وشيت وهرمس. اي ادريس المثلث بالنعمة عليهم السلام. ولهم امور اخر لايسع كتابنا هذا ذكرها ليلا

ذكرها ليلا يخرج عن مقصودنا. واما الطايفة الثالثة وهم الاشراقيون اولاد اخت هرمس المثلث. المسمي باللغة اليونانية طريسيجيسطموس ثووسليوس فاختلطت انسا بهم ببعض الاغراب. فعرف بعض الناس اصطلاحهم. وفك رموزهم. ووصل الينا جملة من علومهم وفضايلهم وغيرها. واما الطايفة الرابعة وهم المشاون الذين اولاد الاغراب المختلطين بنسل الهرامسة. وهم الذين ابتدوا بعبادة اصنام الصور النجومية. وتركوا عبادة الاه الالهية جل جلاله ولا اله غيره. ومن هنا تفرقوا. فالذي وصل البنا من هذين الطايفتين اي الاشراقية والمشايية. فافهم مايرد

اليك

اليك من الاسرار وكنوز الدخاير القديمة الهرمسية. التي لم يسمع بمثلها. ولم احد يسمع بكشفها. ولم حصلت هذه الاشيا الابكد. ومال عظيم. وزمان طويل. واسفار مديدة. فعليك ايها الواصل الي هذه الكنوز بحفظها وكتمها و صونها بغاية الجهد والاخفا. ولا توقف عليها الا لحكما العارفين. والعلما الواصلين. وقد حان لنا ان نشرع في المقصود الذي وعدنا بذكره في هذه المرتبة انشا الله تعالي.

في ذكر الاشكال النباتية فافهم

| شجر | كرم | نخل | شجر مثمر | شجر بلا ثمر | نبات |

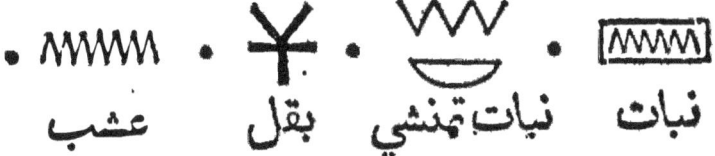

عشب . نبات تمشي . بقل . نبات

شجرة الخطمي . شجرة قاتل . شجرة ترياقي . شجرة الزيتون . نبات السدر . نبات

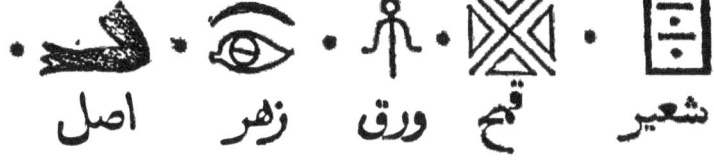

اصل . شعير . زهر . ورق . قمح . شعير

سرو . ورد . يبروح . بزر . اثل . ورد

رمان عنب . خوخ . ثمر . فاكهة . جوز

سنبل · ريحان · رياحين · سفرجل · رمان

عالم · حي · هندبه · عودهندي · قرنفل · أكليل الملك

بادزهر · عودالبرق · دارصيني · دهن النبات · عدس

بلسان · ترياق · دوا · مركب حار

حلو · كثيف · لطيف · يابس · رطب · بارد

حلو	مر	حامض	محلل	مقطع
جلاء	مقوي	منقي	جيد	معتدل
حريف	مجفف	تقطير	تصعيد	تنكيس
حل	تعفين	تكليس	سحق	دق
مخل	مزج	دهن	تصفية	غلي

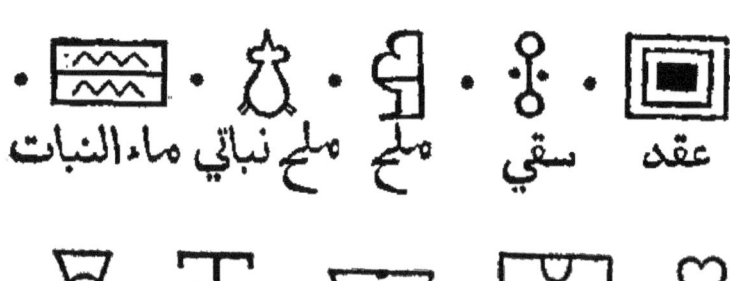

عقد . ملح . ملح نباتي . ماء النبات . سقي . ملح

دهن الزيتون . تفاح . طرفا . عصارة . خل

كسفرة . تمسم . دروبج . عسل نحل . صبر

مرّ . زعفران . سندروس . ماميتا . صمغ

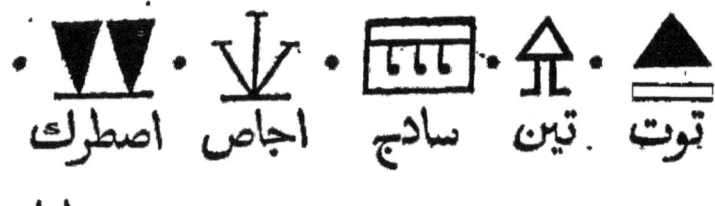

توت لبان . تين . سادج . اجاص . اصطرك

١٠٦

لبان · غالية · مسك · عنبر · لادن

زفت · نبط · حسك · من · مومیا

مرزنجوش · غار · غاریقون · سداب · نفرمر

بصل · كتان · قطن · حرير · ضومران

غافت · سكر · سيكران · خولنجان · بابونج · قنطريون

قنطريون   سعد   مازريون

تمت الاشكال النباتية التي اطلعنا عليها في كتب القوم . وقد آن لنا ان نذكر الاشكال المعدنية ان شاء الله تعالي . وهذه الاشكال كلها مضبوطة محررة كما رأيناه

المرتبة الثالثة في ذكر صور الاشكال المعدنية التي اصطلح عليها الهرامسة الاشراقية والمشايخ. وقد ذكرها دوشام الكاهن في كتابه الذي وضعه في خواص النبات والاحجار المعدنية . وجعله خاصاً مكتوباً بهذا القلم . فاعلم ذلك واكتمه فانه من الاسرار المخزونة .

في صور الا

في صور الإشكال المعدنية

جوهر	معدن ذهب	حجر	فضه	ذهب	معدن

مغنيسيا	نحاس	مها	زيبق	حجرالسم

توتية	طلق	نحاسي مرقشيتا	مرقشيتا ذهبي

رهج اسرنج	مامعدني	انتيمون	اسرب	مغناطيس

بورق	جوهر الحديد	حديد	رهج	
رماد	كلس	طين محرق	طين	
قلي	مكلس	حديد	برماهن	صلب	اسفيداج
بوريطش	زنجار	نطرون	شب	باروق
فيروزج	بلخش	قصدير	طرطير	طلق
				زاج

ياقوت ، تنكار ، جزع ، بورق ، زاج

مرجان ، لازورد ، زمرد ، كدان ، عقيق

زرنيخ لحم ، زرنيخ ، فحم ، نوشادر ، نورة

طين احمر ، طين ابيض ، زجاج اصفر ، رهج ، حجر جبسين ، حجر اخضر

زبرجد ، كبريت ، صخر ، حجر اصفر ، خماهان ، يشم

١١١

شاذنه صوان سنباذج دهنج بشم

حجرالحيه قير الماس مجمره سلسله حديد

حجرشفاف قطع حك حل نقش
الحجر الحجر الحجر الحجر

حجرالسبج شنج حلزون حجرهندي حجرالرحا

حجرروخو حجرالماء فخار انية من ساير ما
يستعمل من المعادن
كل واحد يعرف برسمه

بيره مصنوع

بیر مصنوع خارصینی زیبق   سحق ترکیب حجر
معقود   الاحجار مع حجر

حجر رخام   تکلیس   حجر البادزهر   مغناطیس
الفضه   الاحجار

حجر الدم   حجر الخطاف   حجر المطر   ملح جبلی

حجر النفط   قبسور   حجر سماوی   حجر المیه   کحل

اثمد. الت القطع کسر و خرق صلایه و فهر کتابة الحجر
الما الخارق

الماء الخارق   هندسة
في الحجر   الاحجار

تمت الاشكال الهرمسية التي وجدناها واطلعنا عليها. والتي لم تعرف حقيقتها لم نذكرناها. وربما يجعلون للشكل الواحد معنيين او ثلثة فاكثر بحسب الاصطلاع. لان كل طايفة منهم لها علامة في كل شي وبها يميزوابه عن غير أبناء جنسهم. فلا يختلط معهم غيرهم والله الموفق الي الخير.
تم

الخاتمة

الخاتمة الفريدة

في ذكر اقلام ادعت طايفة من قوم النبط والكلدانيين والصابية. انها كانت تستعمل قبل الطوفان.

فاول قلم شيشيم الذي كتب به الصحف علي طين الحكمة. واحرقه بالنار فصار فخاراً وهو هذا القلم المبارك كما تراه.

صفت

ا ب ج د هـ و ز ح ط

ي ك ل م ن ذ س ع ف

ص ق ر ش ت ث خ ذ ض

ظ غ

وهذا

وهذا ايضًا قلم قديم تزعم فراعنة مصر انه كان يستعمل قبل الطوفان . وكانوا يتبركون به . ويكتبون بهذا القلم كتب دعواتهم التي يقرونها في هياكلهم قدام اصنامهم . وقد رايت بارض الصعيد نواويسًا وبرايٍ واحجارًا مرقومة بهذا القلم . فيحتمل ان يكون ذلك صحيحًا كما ذكروه . و تبعت في ذلك راي النبط و الكلدانيين وهذه صفة حروفه

وامّا الاقلام

واما الاقلام التي اشتهرت بين الامم الماضية القديمة والحادثة باتفاق ارايهم جميعاً. ان لاقلام كانت ثلثة اقلام. وهي القلم السرياني القديم. المعبّر عنه با لقلم الاول الالهي الذي علمه الله تعالي لابينا ادم. عليه السلام. ثم بعده القلم السمائي الذي نزل به صحف شيت عليه السلام. ثم بعده قلم ادريس الذي نزل به جبريل عليه السلام. وهذا راي الجمهور المتفق عليه من ساير الملك والاديان والدليل علي صحة ذلك ماذكره خنوخا في الاسفار التي ذكرها. وحقق هذا الكلام ايضاً اغاديمون بقوله في سفر الحقايا مما يجب علي اصحاب النواميس الالهية. ان يثبتوا اسرارهم بهذه الاقلام الثلاثة. فاستد للنا بقول هذا الفاضل صحة هذا الكلام. ورسمنا شكل

شكل الاقلام علي راية واعتماده . فافهم ترشد الي الصواب .

صفة القلم السرياني علي رأي القدماء من الحكما علي هذا الوضع والشكل كما ترى .

ا ب ج د هـ و ز ح ط

ي ك ل م ن س ع ف ت

ص ق ر ش ت

اعلم ان

اعلم ان هذا الوضع علي الرسم القديم . واما في زماننا هذا . فقد وضعوه علي صورة اخري يخالفها في بعض اشكال الحروف كما ترى . وهذه صفته.

فهذا

فهذا هو القلم الذي كتب علي عهد ادم عليه السلام . واما من قال انه خلاف هذا فهو زورو بهتان وتزييف . والله اعلم بالصواب .

صفة قلم شيثيم الذي تعلمه بالوجي من الله تعالي. وهو ايضاً مختلف فيه علي اربع روايات. فالاول منها علي راي الهرامسة. والثاني علي راي النبط. والثالث علي راي الصابية. والرابع علي راي الكلدانية . وهولاءهم الامم القديمه التي اخذت عنهم ساير الامم الحادثة بعدهم الي يومنا هذا .

وهذه صفته علي راي الهرامسة

ا	ٮ	ٮ	ٮ	ٮ	٦٦	ٮ
	ي	ق	غ	ب	ك	ر

ج

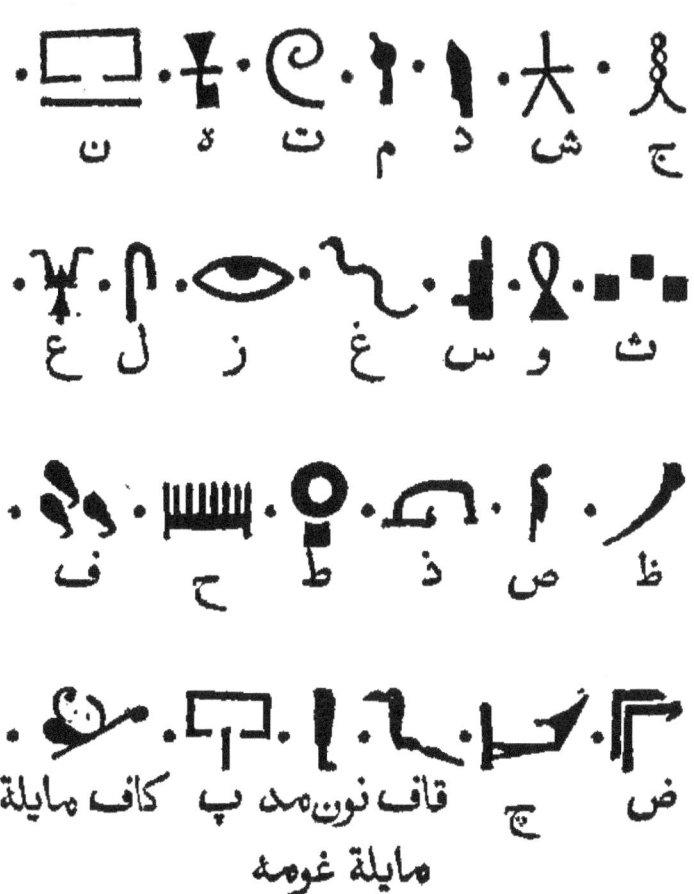

ظازابية

⊙ . ᛋ . ᛋ . 𓀀 . 🏛 .

هاهمزية جيم مد جزم مع الزا زا عجمية
غومة   مدغوم

واما كيفية قراته بقاعدة اصطلاحهم . ايهوم .
يووق . قاا . غيوا . بيدم . كاغيج . رون . جهوم .
شاء . دنز . مايب . تنرس . هين . ثاند . ووآود .
سپرم . خيوري . زيد . لوغف . عي . ظيوم .
صيقام . ذلپ . طقر . حيست . فيست . ضمنز
جل . ڤم . نيمْ . پپ . كأل . ظيمپ . هام . جِپلت .
جرز . ژايغ . فهذه جملة حروفه وعدتها ثمانية
وثلاثين حرفاً . لان فيها حروف لاتوجد في اللسان
العربي والعجمي الآن يكون علماً بلسانهم واصطلاحهم
و

و هوايضاً بخلاف قاعدة ابجد وغيرها . بل مرتبتهم علي حسب نطق لسانهم علي هيئة ما وضعوه . فافهم ترشد . واما قاعدة النبط فانهم قوم اكثر ما يفتمدون عليه في اشكال الحروف علي صور للحيوان . ويرتبونه بحسب الوضع الطبيعي . ويقولون ان كل شكل صورة تدل علي اسرار ما خفي من بواطنها مثال ذلك اذا ارادوا ان يصفوا ملكًا شجاعًا ذو هيبة ومكر وبخل . يجعلون صورة انسان راسه كراس اسد. وبين يديه ذيب يشير اليه باصبع واحد . وان ارادوا وصفه بالعقل والذكا والفطنة والحكمة . جعلوا صورة انسان راسه كراس الفيل . وهو يشير باصبعه الي قرد جالس . وان ارادوا صفه بالعدل والكرم والجود . جعلوا صورة انسان راسه كراس

كراس طاير باسط يديه . وبين يديه صورة برج الميزان . وصورة الشمس والقمر . وان ارادوا وصفه بالظلم والجهل وعدم السياسة والديانة . جعلوا صورة انسان راسه كراس كلب اوخنزير اوحمار. وبين يديه انية فيها نار . وصورة سيف اوفاس. واذا ارادوا وصف انسان بالسقم و الضعف والمرض . يجعلوا صورة لضف انسان . ومن خلفه هذه الاشكال .

ثم يرسموا من قدامه صورة صنم زحل اوشكله مع هذه الاشكال .

واذا ارادوا وصف انسان مات بالقتل . يصوروا صورة انسان راسه كراس خفاش . اوكراس بوم . ويجعلون

ويجعلون خلفه صورة عقرب مع هذا الحرف . ⋀⋀⋀ . وقدامه صورة شيطان مع هذه الاشكال .

واذا ارادوا وصف انسان مات مسموماً . فانهم يجعلون صورة انسان راسه كالسرطان او كراس السلحفاه . وبين يديه انية او قدح من زجاج . مع هذاه الاشكال .

واذا ارادوا وصف انسان مات بالوباء . او بالحمي المحرقة . او يمرض من مفسدات الدم ومحرقات الاخلاط . يجعلون صورة انسان جالس علي كرسي . و بيده سهم . وفوق راسة تعبان ملتف علي عنق كرسي . وكدامه هذه الاشكال .

واذا ارادوا وصف انسان بالجاه والعز وسعة الوقت وطيب الحال . فانهم يجعلون صورة انسان ويده كرة . او صولنجان . او دايرة . وعلي راسه ثلج وقدامه عقاب ومن خلفه كلب وهذه الاشكال مرسومه بدايرهم .

واذا ارادوا وصف انسان بالعقل والحكمة والديانة . وهو تام في كل اموره . ليس فيه ما يكره من جميع الوجوه . فانهم يجعلون صورة انسان حسن الوجه . وله جناحان علي هية الملايكة . وبيده سفريط العه . وقد سيف وميزان . وخلفه

وخلفه اناان احدهما ملان ماء.. والاخر نار ممتو قد. وتحت رجله اليمين كرة قد رسم عليها شكل السرطان وتحت رجله الشمال صورة اناء عميق. وفيه حيات وعقارب وانواع الدبيب. وهو مغطي بغطاء راسه كراس العقاب. فانظر يا ولدي الي هولاء القوم وما قد وضعوه من الرموز والاشكال التي لم يعرفها سواهم. وقد رايت في بربا هرمس صورة مجلس. وهو هيكل السيد دواناي الذي خاطبه الثمس والقمر. وصورة ذلك انهم وضعوا هيئة تابوت السر. قد نقش بانواع الصور العجيبة والاشكال الغريبة. وصنعوا علي التابوت كرماً قد بنتت وعرشت عليه. والسيد قايم فوق التابوت. وبيده عصا قد نبتت في اسفلها شجره خطمي. وهي ملتفة عليه. وخلفه صورة يير

يبرتتقد بالنار. و اربعة من الملايكة ياخذون الحيّات و العقارب و انواع الحشرات فيلقونها في ذلك النير النار. وفوق راسه تاج مكلل بالغار وعلي يمينه الشمس. وعلي شماله القمر. وبيده خاتم فيه صور البروج الاثني عشر. و قدام التابوت صورة شجرة الزيتون قد نبتت وعليها انواع وتحت انواع الحيوان. وعلي بعد يسير صورة جبل عالٍ. وعليه سبع منابر من ذهب. وفوقهم صورة السما. وقد مُدَّ منها يد وخرج منه النور. وهو يشير با صبعه الي شجرة الزيتون. وصورة انسان راسه في السما وجله في الارض. قد غلّت يداه و رجلاه وبين يدين السيد سبعة مجامر. وكندرتان. وانا قد ملي بشيّ من البنات العطر. وقدرة طويلة العنق ملآنة بالاصطرك

بالاصطرك . والنهار بشكله تحت رجله اليمني .
والليل بشكله تحت رجله اليسرى . وقد وضع
قدامه على كرسي عال مصحف الميدوم الاكبر.
وفيه صور الافلاك وأسمايها . والكواكب والبروج
والمنازل والدرج . وكلما في الفلك الاعلى من
الهيآت كلها . وحق قدمىلى نصفه طين . ونصفه
الآخر رمل . وسراج معلق يتقد دايماً . وشى
من الثمر . ومن ثم السدر والزيتون . في اناء من
الزبرجد . خلف السفر . ولوح من كدان اسود
فيه سبعة اسطر . وصفة العناصر الاربعة . وانسان
حامل رجل ميت . وكلب فوق اسد . فانظر
يا اخي الى هذه الرموز التي هي مفاتيح خزاين
الكنوز . وما قد احتوت عليه من اسرار علوم

الأولين

الاولين و الاخرين . الذي يكل كل عارف عن معرفة جزءٌ فكيف كله . وعلي هذا القياس لا يمكن الاحتياط بكلية امورهم . وانما وضعنا وذكرنا اموراً بحيث للحكيم العارف بمادي الاشيا وغاياتها . وعللها وحركاتها . وتنقلاتها وادوارها . يدرك البعض بالبعض . فيتصل بمعرفته الي خفايا اسرار العالم . وفي هذا القدر كفايه لمن كان له قلب والقي السمع وهو شهيد . وهذا صفة القلم الذي اوعدنا كما تراه . وهو من جملة اقلامهم المكتومة .

ا . ب . ج . د . ه . و . ز . ح . ط

ك . ل . م . ن . س . ع . ف . ص . ق

ر . ش . ت . ث . خ . ذ . ض . ظ . غ

وهذا

وهذا صفة قلم الصابية. وهم اصحاب الرصودات والطلسمات والاسرار والنارنجات الخارقة وذكر اغاذيمون انه نقل العلوم الطلسمية عنه. ولم يسبقهم الي ذلك احد من المتقدمين و المتاخرين. فافهم ذلك. وهذا قلمهم.

ا . ب . ج . د . ه‍ . و . ز

ح . ط . ي . ك . ل . م . ن . س . ع

ف . ص . ق . ر . ش . ت . ث . خ

ذ . ض . ظ . غ

واما

واما الكلدانيين فكانوا اعلم الناس في زمانهم بالعلوم والمعارف والحكم والصنايع. وكانوا الاكراد الاول يريدون مناظرتهم ومماثلتهم. ولكن شتان مابين الثري والثريا. وانما كانت براعة الاكراد الاول في صناعة الفلاحة وخواص النبات. يدعون انهم من اولاد بيذوشاد. و قد وصل اليهم سفر الفلاحة لادم عليه السلام. وسفر صفريث. وسفر قوثامي. وعلي كل حال انهم يدعون معرفة الاسفار السبعة. ومصحف السيد دواناي. ويدعون السحر و الطلسم و ليس كذلك. بل ما وصلت لهم هذه العلوم والفنون آلا من الكلدانيين. وهم المقدمين عليهم فيها. ولذلك

كانت

كانت عداوة باينة مسمرة بينهم . وهذا صفة قلم الكلدانيين القديم .

ا	ب	ج	د	هـ	و	ز	ح	ط

ي	ك	ل	م	ن	س	ع	ف	ب

ت	ش	ر	ق	ص

صفة

www.ingramcontent.com/pod-product-compliance
Lightning Source LLC
Chambersburg PA
CBHW040056200426
43193CB00060B/2938